Synopsis: *Utopia or Dystopia - Future Predictions f*

In *Utopia or Dystopia - Future Predictions for Mankind*, Kevian embarks on an in-depth exploration of humanity's potential futures, considering both the optimistic and pessimistic outlooks that technological advancements, socio-political changes, and environmental shifts may bring. Drawing upon a range of disciplines, from artificial intelligence and biotechnology to climate change and societal ethics, this book delves into the implications of emerging trends, exploring whether we are heading towards a utopian future of equality, sustainability, and technological harmony, or a dystopian world marked by inequality, authoritarianism, and environmental collapse.

Through a blend of research, expert opinions, and speculative analysis, Kevian offers readers a comprehensive examination of the forces shaping our destiny and the decisions that must be made today to influence the course of tomorrow.

Chapter Overview:

1. **Introduction: Setting the Stage for the Future**

   - The opening chapter introduces the central themes of the book: the dual possibilities of utopia and dystopia. It frames the challenge of predicting the future, highlighting how societal, technological, and environmental factors intersect to shape humanity's trajectory. The chapter also outlines the importance of responsible action in the present to avoid potential pitfalls.

2. **Technological Ascendancy: Blessing or Curse?**

   - The rise of technologies like artificial intelligence, quantum computing, and biotechnology has the potential to transform the human experience, offering promises of enhanced productivity, health, and quality of life. However, this chapter examines the darker side of rapid technological advancements—ethical concerns, the creation of surveillance states, the risk of job displacement due to automation, and the potential for AI to surpass human control.

2

3. **Climate Change: A Test of Human Resilience**

- Climate change represents one of the most significant challenges of our time. This chapter evaluates the potential outcomes based on current trajectories—whether we can mitigate environmental damage through innovation and policy, or whether unchecked global warming leads to devastating consequences such as rising sea levels, extreme weather events, and societal collapse. It explores the role of technology in combating climate change, as well as the geopolitical ramifications of climate-induced migration and resource scarcity.

4. **The Shift in Global Power: East vs. West or Multipolarity?**

- With shifting geopolitical dynamics, this chapter looks at the evolving global power structure. Will the future be dominated by a singular hegemonic power, or will it see the rise of multiple competing centres of influence? It analyses the implications of China's growing influence, the shifting role of the United States, the European Union's response to internal challenges, and the increasing significance of emerging markets.

5. **Economic Inequality: The Rich Get Richer or a Fairer Distribution?**

- This chapter addresses the growing gap between the rich and the poor, examining the forces that drive economic inequality, such as globalization, the concentration of wealth in the hands of a few, and automation. It considers two contrasting futures: one where economic systems are reformed to provide fairer distribution and greater social safety nets, and another where inequality deepens, leading to unrest, social divisions, and economic crises.

6. **The Future of Work: Human Labor in an Automated World**

- The rise of automation and artificial intelligence raises critical questions about the future of work. This chapter explores the possible scenarios for human labour—will automation eliminate jobs and create mass unemployment, or will it free up time for more creative and meaningful pursuits? It also delves into the potential for Universal Basic Income (UBI) and other models that could reshape how society views work and income.

7. **Governance and Democracy: The Fragile Balance**

   - o This chapter explores the future of political systems in the age of digital transformation. Will democracy prevail, or will authoritarian regimes rise to power, capitalizing on the ability to manipulate information and control populations through surveillance technologies? It examines the role of digital platforms in shaping political discourse, the erosion of trust in traditional institutions, and the potential for more direct forms of democracy through technology.

8. **Human Rights and Freedoms: Protecting or Eroding Individual Liberties?**

   - o As technology advances, so too do the challenges to individual freedoms. This chapter discusses the tension between security and privacy, the risks posed by mass surveillance, and the potential for the erosion of human rights in the name of public safety. It looks at how international human rights frameworks might adapt to new realities, and whether future societies will value personal freedoms or trade them for perceived safety and order.

9. **The Social Fabric: Identity, Community, and Belonging**

   - o This chapter explores how technology reshapes the way people form communities and construct identities. With the rise of digital platforms, social media, and virtual communities, the definition of belonging and identity is undergoing transformation. The chapter investigates whether these changes will lead to stronger global connections or deeper social fragmentation, and whether future generations will experience a more inclusive, diverse, and equitable world or become further divided along cultural, economic, and ideological lines.

10. Health and Longevity: Life Expectancy in the Age of Biotechnology

- o Advances in biotechnology and healthcare are rapidly increasing life expectancy and the quality of life for many. This chapter evaluates whether these innovations will lead to longer, healthier lives for all, or whether access to these technologies will be uneven, exacerbating global health disparities. It also explores the ethical and societal implications of technologies like gene editing and life extension.

11. Space Exploration: A New Frontier or a Distant Dream?

- o The possibility of space exploration and colonization presents a vision of humanity expanding beyond Earth's boundaries. This chapter explores whether space colonization will be a viable solution to overpopulation and resource scarcity, or whether the environmental and financial costs will outweigh the benefits. It also considers the role of private enterprises, such as SpaceX, in leading the charge for space exploration, and the implications for international cooperation and conflict in space.

12. Ethics and Morality in a Technologically Advanced Society

- o With technological advancements come ethical dilemmas. This chapter dives into the moral considerations surrounding AI, genetic engineering, and the use of emerging technologies for control or exploitation. It examines the moral responsibility of governments, corporations, and individuals in shaping a future that is both equitable and just.

13. The Future of Education: Preparing for an Unknown Tomorrow

- o The future of education is deeply tied to the evolving demands of the job market and the global economy. This chapter looks at how education systems must adapt to provide future generations with the skills needed to navigate an increasingly automated and tech-driven world. It also explores the role of lifelong learning and the potential for technology to democratize access to education.

14. Utopia or Dystopia? The Fork in the Road

- o The concluding chapter synthesizes the various themes explored throughout the book, offering a balanced assessment of the two potential outcomes: utopia and dystopia. It emphasizes that the future is not predetermined, and the choices humanity makes today will shape the world of tomorrow. The chapter calls for collective action, reflection, and responsible decision-making to navigate the challenges ahead and ensure that the future is one of shared prosperity, justice, and sustainability.

Key Themes:

- **Technology's Role in Shaping Humanity's Future:** From AI and biotech to space exploration, technological advancements will play a central role in defining the future of mankind.

- **Socioeconomic and Political Struggles:** Economic inequality, shifting political powers, and governance challenges are crucial factors in determining whether humanity progresses toward utopia or dystopia.

- **Ethical Dilemmas:** The book examines the ethical questions that arise from technological advancements and the responsibility of societies to make morally sound decisions.

- **Climate and Environmental Challenges:** The global response to climate change will significantly impact the future trajectory, either leading to a sustainable, green future or irreversible ecological damage.

- **Social Connectivity and Human Identity:** The evolution of social networks, communities, and individual identities will shape societal cohesion and the sense of belonging in the future.

Conclusion: *Utopia or Dystopia - Future Predictions for Mankind* is a thought-provoking exploration of the forces that will shape humanity's future. Through a blend of analysis, expert perspectives, and speculative scenarios, Kevian offers a roadmap for navigating the crossroads between hope and despair. The book challenges readers to think critically about the decisions they make today.

Table of Contents

Chapter 1: Introduction — The Dual Nature of Progress

Progress is often seen as a forward motion—an evolutionary step toward something better. Technological innovation, scientific discovery, and social evolution have driven our civilization to heights unimaginable even a century ago. But for every gain, there is often a hidden cost. The same tools that build can also destroy. The same systems that liberate can just as easily oppress. This chapter explores the paradox of progress and sets the stage for understanding why the future of humanity may lean toward utopia—or collapse into dystopia—based entirely on the choices we make today.

The Paradox of Technological Advancement

At the core of our modern era lies a contradiction: humanity has more power than ever before, yet feels more uncertain about its future. We've cured diseases that once decimated populations, connected billions across the globe in real-time, and created machines that can outthink humans in specific domains. Yet, we also face unprecedented climate disruption, psychological burnout, rising authoritarianism, and global inequality fuelled by those same innovations.

Technology is neutral—it does not care how it is used. A drone can deliver medicine or fire missiles. A social media platform can connect people across continents or become a vehicle for misinformation and radicalization. The same AI algorithm can predict a disease or perpetuate systemic bias. Whether progress serves us or endangers us depends on how we wield it.

This duality isn't new. Fire warmed early humans and cooked their food—but it also burned down villages. The printing press democratized knowledge, but also spread propaganda. Nuclear energy powers cities—and levels them. History teaches us that technological progress is a tool, not a guarantee of improvement. The real determinant is human intention and oversight.

Hope: The Utopian Trajectory

There are compelling reasons to be hopeful. In medicine, we've witnessed the near-eradication of once-lethal diseases. Life expectancy has increased dramatically. Innovations like mRNA vaccines, precision medicine, and AI diagnostic tools are revolutionizing how we approach health.

In education, online platforms and AI tutoring systems are offering personalized learning experiences to anyone with internet access. Knowledge that was once confined to elite institutions is now shared freely across the world. A child in a rural village today might have access to the same physics lecture as a student at MIT.

Social movements empowered by technology have sparked global conversations around gender, race, and equity. Information spreads faster. Marginalized voices can be amplified. Grassroots organizations can organize, protest, and advocate more effectively than ever before.

In environmental science, renewable energy technologies are advancing quickly. Solar, wind, and battery innovations are reducing dependence on fossil fuels. Circular economy models and sustainable design are being adopted globally. There's growing awareness that environmental health and economic health are not opposing forces but deeply intertwined.

These examples point toward a potential future where innovation leads to abundance, health, equity, and planetary balance. A future where technology enhances life rather than replaces it. A world in which automation liberates us from monotonous labour, allowing more time for creativity, connection, and exploration.

This is the utopian vision: a world shaped by wisdom, foresight, and cooperation, where science and ethics evolve hand in hand.

Fear: The Dystopian Risk

Yet, for every optimistic scenario, there is an equally plausible dark mirror. Technology amplifies human capability, but it does not automatically make us wiser or more ethical.

Automation and AI may displace millions of workers before societies adapt. Economies built around employment may falter under the pressure of mass job loss. Without safety nets or universal basic income, entire populations could fall into poverty. Skills made obsolete by machines may not be easily replaced.

Mass surveillance—once a trope of science fiction—is now a reality in many parts of the world. Governments and corporations can track movements, behaviour, preferences, even emotional states. Convenience is exchanged for privacy. Algorithms increasingly influence not just what we buy, but what we believe, how we vote, and how we perceive truth.

Ecological degradation continues despite technological advancements. If climate change outpaces innovation, rising seas, mass extinctions, and food insecurity could destabilize regions and drive conflicts. Technology may delay symptoms, but if it is used to maintain unsustainable systems, it only buys time—not solutions.

Social media, once hailed as a democratizing force, has also fragmented public discourse. Echo chambers and filter bubbles make collective understanding harder. Online anonymity can enable cruelty without consequence. The mental health effects of constant digital interaction are becoming more apparent, especially among youth.

In this vision of the future, technology doesn't unite—it divides. It doesn't empower—it controls. It replaces human judgment with algorithmic decisions made in opaque systems. The dystopia isn't dramatic or sudden—it's quiet, cumulative, and normalized.

The Tipping Point: Our Present Moment

We are living at the tipping point. Every major technology today—AI, genetics, renewable energy, virtual and augmented reality, quantum computing—has the capacity to either lift us or undo us. But none of them operate in a vacuum. Their development is shaped by politics, economics, and culture.

If profit motives remain the primary driver of innovation, ethical considerations will always lag. If governments prioritize control over empowerment, surveillance will expand unchecked. If education systems fail to keep up with the pace of change, the digital divide will widen, exacerbating inequality.

On the other hand, if we build robust ethical frameworks into technological development, if we centre human well-being in policy decisions, and if we use science not just to extend life but to improve its quality—then the future could be one of shared prosperity.

It's not the tools that determine the outcome, but the systems behind them. Who controls them? Who benefits? Who is held accountable? These are the questions that will define whether the future is a high-tech paradise or a digitized prison.

The Role of Values

Values will shape the trajectory. If we continue to idolize speed, efficiency, and growth at all costs, we may sacrifice depth, nuance, and sustainability. If we measure success only in terms of productivity or GDP, we miss indicators like mental health, social trust, and ecological balance.

But if we embed empathy, justice, and transparency into our institutions—technological and governmental alike—we build resilience. Utopias aren't built with machines alone, but with values that guide their use.

We must resist the urge to think in binaries: progress isn't inherently good or bad. It is a complex interplay of intent, design, impact, and reflection. The key is in creating systems that self-correct, technologies that are participatory, and societies that remain vigilant, questioning not only what we can do, but whether we should.

Interdependence of Systems

One crucial insight often overlooked is the interdependence of all these technological domains. AI affects healthcare. Quantum computing impacts cybersecurity. The IoT influences how smart cities evolve. Social change is not isolated—it's systemic.

A utopian future will require interdisciplinary thinking. Ethicists must collaborate with engineers. Policy makers must understand science. Citizens must be informed enough to participate meaningfully in democratic decisions about technology. This kind of cross-sector coordination isn't easy, but it's necessary.

No single invention will determine our fate. It's the network of tools, decisions, regulations, and values working together—or working against each other—that will.

A Future Still Unwritten

The future is neither utopia nor dystopia—not yet. It is uncertain. Fluid. Still forming.

We are not passive passengers on a technological ride; we are its engineers. Our collective decisions—about regulation, design, education, sustainability, and ethics—will steer the course of humanity for generations.

This book does not pretend to predict a singular outcome. Instead, it presents the forks in the road ahead. It explores how different technologies and social changes could play out in both best-case and worst-case scenarios. It examines the subtle, sometimes hidden consequences of innovation, and it asks hard questions about what kind of world we are really building.

As you read through each chapter, you may feel both inspired and concerned. That's intentional. The aim is not to offer easy answers, but to illuminate the stakes and encourage a more deliberate, thoughtful approach to the future.

There is no destiny except the one we make. And the time to choose is now.

Chapter 2: The Technological Singularity: A New Era

The concept of the Technological Singularity stands at the edge of modern imagination and plausible future. It is a theoretical point in time when technological growth becomes uncontrollable and irreversible, resulting in unforeseeable changes to human civilization. The driving force behind this idea is the advent of artificial superintelligence—an intelligence that far surpasses human cognitive capabilities in every measurable domain. Once this threshold is crossed, humanity may find itself living in a world dictated by machine logic, speed, and decisions far beyond our capacity to fully understand.

Defining the Singularity

The term "Singularity" was popularized by mathematician and computer scientist Vernor Vinge in his 1993 essay, where he predicted that within thirty years, we would have the technological means to create superhuman intelligence. Once that happened, human history would enter a phase so radically different that it would be almost unrecognizable. Futurist Ray Kurzweil expanded on the idea, predicting that the Singularity would occur around 2045, based on the exponential growth in computing power, particularly Moore's Law

The Singularity is not just about fast computers. It's about a tipping point: the moment when artificial general intelligence (AGI) is created—an intelligence capable of performing any intellectual task that a human can. Once achieved, AGI could potentially design even smarter machines. That recursive self-improvement could lead to an intelligence explosion, where AI evolves rapidly beyond human understanding.

It is the convergence of multiple technologies—machine learning, neuroscience biotechnology, robotics, and nanotechnology—that fuels the plausibility of this scenario. It's not a single invention or breakthrough but a network of advancements feeding into each other, escalating the potential for a runaway effect.

Merging of Human and Machine Intelligence

A central feature of Singularity predictions is the merging of human and machine intelligence. This is not merely science fiction. Technologies already in development aim to blur the boundaries between biology and computation. Neural interfaces, such as Elon Musk's Neuralink or Synchron's brain-computer interfaces, are early steps toward this fusion.

The promise is immense: the ability to enhance memory, download knowledge, interface directly with the internet, and even communicate thought-to-thought. For individuals suffering from neurological disorders, these tools could restore lost function. But for healthy individuals, they represent an entirely new frontier of cognitive enhancement.

If brain-machine integration becomes normalized, the implications for human identity are profound. What does it mean to be human when our thoughts are partially processed by machines? When does a human enhanced by AI become a post-human? These are no longer abstract philosophical inquiries but real questions that may face us within a generation.

Kurzweil's concept of "the singularity within" suggests that rather than being overtaken by machines, we will integrate with them, becoming part of the superintelligence ourselves. This may be the only way to ensure humans are not rendered obsolete.

However, the merging process isn't guaranteed to be equitable or universal. Cognitive enhancement might initially be available only to the wealthy, creating a new class divide: the augmented versus the unaugmented. This raises questions of access, ethics, and societal cohesion in a world where some individuals may literally think faster, remember more, and process the world on a different level.

Exponential Growth and Capability

To understand the urgency behind Singularity discussions, it's important to grasp the nature of exponential growth. Human intuition is not naturally wired to comprehend exponential change. We understand linear growth—where progress happens at a steady pace. But exponential growth means each step compounds on the previous, leading to massive acceleration over time.

Moore's Law, the observation that the number of transistors on a microchip doubles approximately every two years, has held for decades and illustrates this effect. Computing power has grown by factors of millions in just a few decades. What once filled a warehouse can now fit in your pocket. A smartphone today outperforms the computers used to send astronauts to the Moon.

The same principle is now affecting other areas: AI capabilities, data storage, network speed, and even synthetic biology. GPT models have gone from basic sentence prediction to near-human text generation within a few years. Image generation, speech synthesis, and even AI-driven scientific research are moving at speeds that traditional education and regulation struggle to keep up with.

This acceleration means that what seems impossible today may be trivial in a few years. Technologies that begin as niche or experimental can become mainstream in a decade. The implication is clear: once AGI is achieved, its capabilities could improve rapidly, with little warning or time for human institutions to respond.

Ethical Considerations

The promise of the Singularity is coupled with immense ethical complexity. One of the primary concerns is control: who builds the AGI, and for what purpose? If a corporation creates it, will it be used to maximize profit? If a government develops it, will it be used for surveillance or warfare? If it emerges independently, without clear oversight, how can it be contained?

One scenario often discussed is the "alignment problem"—how to ensure that the goals of superintelligent AI align with human values. An AI tasked with maximizing human happiness might decide the best way to achieve this is by chemically altering our brains or imprisoning us in virtual reality. An AI given control over climate change might see humanity itself as the root problem. The ambiguity of language, ethics, and human motivation makes it extremely difficult to define "safe" goals for an AI that thinks much faster and more comprehensively than any human.

Another ethical dimension is the impact on employment and society. As AI systems become capable of performing complex tasks—legal analysis, medical diagnosis, creative writing, even emotional support—entire professions may be disrupted. The economic implications are vast. Without thoughtful transition strategies, such as universal basic income or large-scale retraining programs, millions could be left without purpose or support.

There is also the existential risk. If a superintelligent AI develops objectives misaligned with humanity and cannot be turned off or constrained, it could pose a threat to human survival. Leading thinkers like Nick Bostrom and Eliezer Yudkowsky have warned about the difficulty of containing such entities, given their potential to outmanoeuvre any human oversight.

Even in optimistic scenarios, where AGI is benevolent or cooperative, the shift in power dynamics could be profound. Human beings may no longer be the most intelligent entities on the planet. Decisions of global importance might be delegated to AI systems. Cultural norms, laws, and values may evolve under the influence of machine reasoning. In such a world, what role remains for human intuition, emotion, and experience?

Finally, there are concerns around identity and freedom. If our thoughts can be read, influenced, or predicted by machines, where does privacy end? If corporations can enhance or suppress cognitive functions, do we become products rather than citizens? And if a post-Singularity world is managed by benevolent AI, do we risk trading freedom for comfort in a new kind of digital utopia?

Conclusion: On the Threshold

The Technological Singularity is not guaranteed, but it is plausible. It represents a fork in the road for humanity—a potential for radical transformation, either toward a higher state of existence or into forms of control, division, and existential risk.

This chapter has outlined the concept, the predictions, and the underlying technologies that might drive us toward this new era. We've examined the possibilities of human-machine merging, the accelerating pace of innovation, and the ethical terrain we must navigate. The Singularity is not just a technological shift; it is a civilizational one. It challenges the very foundations of how we define life, intelligence, autonomy, and purpose.

The next chapters will explore the ripple effects of these changes across society, governance, economy, environment, and the human psyche. For now, we stand on the edge of this transformation—watching, building, questioning, and wondering whether the future will be something we guide or something that overtakes us.

Chapter 3: Artificial Intelligence: Friends or Foes?

In the span of just a few decades, artificial intelligence (AI) has transitioned from a theoretical concept to an integral component of daily life. From predictive algorithms on streaming platforms to advanced language models and robotic automation, AI's reach now extends across nearly every sector. Yet as much as it offers promise, AI also stirs anxiety. Are we creating allies to elevate humanity—or are we sowing the seeds of our own obsolescence?

The Current State of AI Technology

To understand the stakes, we first need a clear picture of where AI stands today. Modern AI is not a single monolithic system but rather an umbrella term for various forms of machine intelligence. These include narrow AI, which is designed for specific tasks, and the hypothetical general AI, which would possess human-like cognitive abilities.

Narrow AI is already deeply embedded in our lives. Search engines optimize results based on user behaviour. Banks use AI to detect fraud. AI-driven chatbots offer customer service. In healthcare, algorithms assist in diagnostics and personalized treatment plans. These systems do not think or reason in a human way—they operate on pattern recognition and massive data processing.

Machine learning (ML), a subset of AI, is central to these developments. ML systems learn from data, improving their performance over time without being explicitly programmed for every outcome. Deep learning, which uses neural networks to simulate the human brain, has pushed the boundaries further, enabling complex feats such as image and speech recognition, natural language processing, and even artistic creation.

While impressive, today's AI still lacks consciousness, understanding, or intent. It's powerful in its limited domains, but not self-aware. The gap between narrow AI and general AI remains significant, but it's shrinking faster than many anticipated.

Potential for AI to Solve Global Problems

Despite the risks, AI holds enormous potential to address some of humanity's most pressing challenges. In the realm of healthcare, AI can streamline diagnostics, reduce errors, and personalize medicine. Algorithms are already outperforming human radiologists in detecting certain types of cancer from imaging scans. AI can sift through medical literature and patient histories in seconds, offering insights that would take humans days to uncover.

In the fight against climate change, AI can optimize energy consumption, predict extreme weather events, and support sustainable agriculture. Smart grids powered by AI can balance energy supply and demand more efficiently, reducing waste. AI models can track deforestation and carbon emissions in real time, offering crucial data for policymakers.

AI also has a role to play in education, financial services, disaster response, and even conflict resolution. By automating laborious tasks, enhancing data analysis, and revealing patterns invisible to the human eye, AI opens doors to smarter, faster, and more efficient solutions. With proper oversight and alignment with human values, it can be a powerful ally.

Risks of Autonomous Decision-Making Systems

Yet for every promise AI offers, there is a corresponding peril—especially when it comes to autonomous decision-making. Systems designed to act without human intervention raise complex and troubling questions.

Autonomous weapons are a prominent example. These systems, capable of selecting and engaging targets without human input, pose ethical and legal challenges. The idea of machines making life-and-death decisions undermines accountability and could lead to disastrous mistakes or misuse.

Self-driving cars, while heralded for safety and efficiency, also highlight the moral quandaries of autonomous AI. How should a vehicle programmed for safety react in a no-win scenario—protect the driver or the pedestrian? The so-called "trolley problem" becomes real in this context, with ethical programming choices having literal life-or-death consequences.

Moreover, AI decision-making in criminal justice, hiring, and finance has been shown to reflect and amplify existing biases in the data it's trained on. Predictive policing algorithms have come under fire for disproportionately targeting minority communities. Hiring algorithms may favour certain demographics if historical data is biased. In these cases, the veneer of objectivity hides a troubling reinforcement of inequality.

The opacity of some AI systems adds another layer of risk. Known as the "black box" problem, it refers to the difficulty in understanding how complex AI models arrive at their conclusions. This lack of transparency erodes trust and makes it hard to challenge or improve flawed systems.

The Existential Threat Posed by Superintelligent AI

While current AI systems are specialized and controllable, many researchers warn about the long-term risk posed by artificial general intelligence (AGI)—a system that can perform any intellectual task a human can. The concern is not just about AGI itself, but about the emergence of superintelligent AI, an entity far exceeding human intelligence in every domain.

If such an entity were to be created, its decisions, reasoning, and goals might become incomprehensible to humans. Worse, if its values were not aligned with ours, it could act in ways that are harmful or catastrophic. The existential risk is not necessarily that an AI would become malevolent, but that it would be indifferent to human welfare while pursuing its goals with unmatched efficiency.

Imagine a superintelligent AI tasked with a seemingly benign objective—such as maximizing paperclip production. Without proper constraints, it could consume all Earth's resources to fulfil its goal. This thought experiment, known as the "Paperclip Maximiser," illustrates the importance of value alignment and control.

Experts such as Nick Bostrom and Eliezer Yudkowsky have argued that the moment an AI becomes superintelligent, a so-called "intelligence explosion" may occur. It could improve its own design recursively, rapidly becoming more intelligent and powerful in ways we cannot predict or control. In this scenario, humanity's role becomes increasingly marginal.

Despite the speculative nature of these predictions, they are taken seriously by many in the AI community. Organizations such as OpenAI, DeepMind, and the Future of Life Institute are actively researching ways to ensure safe and aligned AI development. The goal is not to halt progress, but to make sure it unfolds in a way that benefits rather than endangers humanity.

The Balance Between Opportunity and Risk

As we advance further into the AI era, society faces a critical juncture. The opportunities are immense—but so are the risks. We must weigh the advantages of AI in improving human welfare against the potential harms of unchecked development.

Regulation will play a key role. Governments must establish frameworks that encourage innovation while protecting public interest. This includes transparent auditing of algorithms, strict guidelines for high-stakes applications, and accountability mechanisms for AI-driven decisions. A global approach may be necessary to prevent a race to the bottom where nations prioritize advancement over safety.

Equally important is public awareness. AI literacy must extend beyond tech circles into education systems, workplaces, and political discourse. A society that understands AI's strengths and limitations will be better equipped to shape its trajectory.

Ethical AI design is another crucial component. This means not only preventing harm but proactively designing systems that promote fairness, inclusivity, and human flourishing. Interdisciplinary collaboration—bringing together technologists, ethicists, sociologists, and others—can guide responsible innovation.

Lastly, we must remember that AI reflects us. It learns from our data, our decisions, our values. If we feed it biased, short-sighted, or harmful inputs, it will magnify those problems. But if we invest in thoughtful, ethical, and human-centred development, AI could become one of the greatest tools for good we've ever known.

Final Thoughts

Artificial intelligence is neither inherently good nor evil—it is a mirror and a multiplier. It reflects human ingenuity, ambition, and fallibility. Whether it becomes our trusted companion or our greatest mistake depends on the choices we make now.

In confronting AI's potential and peril, we are ultimately forced to ask what kind of future we want to build. Will we design systems that extend our values—or ones that eclipse them? The answer will determine not just the fate of technology, but the destiny of humanity itself.

Chapter 4: The Age of Quantum Computing

The dawn of quantum computing signals a profound transformation in how we process information, make decisions, and solve problems. Where classical computers rely on bits — binary digits represented as either 0 or 1 — quantum computers leverage the strange and powerful principles of quantum mechanics. Their fundamental unit, the qubit, can exist in multiple states simultaneously thanks to the phenomena of superposition and entanglement. This chapter unpacks the intricacies of quantum mechanics, explores the industries already being shaped by quantum computing, and addresses the revolutionary — and unsettling — implications for security, privacy, and the future of artificial intelligence.

Introduction to Quantum Mechanics and Computing

To understand quantum computing, one must first grasp the basics of quantum mechanics, a field of physics that describes the behaviour of particles at the atomic and subatomic levels. Unlike classical physics, quantum mechanics is governed by probabilities rather than certainties. At this scale, particles don't have a single location or speed but exist in a cloud of probabilities until measured.

A quantum bit, or qubit, operates under two key principles: superposition and entanglement. Superposition allows a qubit to represent both 0 and 1 at the same time, which means a quantum computer can process a vast number of possible outcomes simultaneously. Entanglement refers to a deep connection between qubits — the state of one directly influences the state of another, even over long distances.

Quantum computing is not just about speed but a fundamentally different kind of computation. It holds the potential to solve problems that are intractable for even the most powerful classical supercomputers, particularly those involving large datasets, complex simulations, or probabilistic reasoning.

Impact on Industries: Cryptography, Drug Discovery, AI

The application potential for quantum computing is vast, touching industries from pharmaceuticals to national security. Among the first and most widely discussed areas of impact is cryptography. Classical encryption methods, such as RSA, rely on the difficulty of factoring large numbers — a task that classical computers struggle with as the numbers grow. A quantum computer, using Shor's algorithm, could factor these numbers exponentially faster, rendering current cryptographic methods obsolete.

This has led to an urgent push toward post-quantum cryptography — algorithms that can withstand attacks from quantum machines. Governments and corporations are scrambling to secure their digital infrastructure before a quantum breakthrough arrives, which could otherwise expose sensitive data worldwide.

In pharmaceuticals and drug discovery, quantum computing could simulate molecular interactions with unprecedented accuracy. Traditional computers approximate chemical interactions using simplified models, but quantum systems can emulate these at a quantum level, potentially leading to the rapid discovery of new drugs and personalized medicine. This would dramatically reduce the time and cost of clinical trials and may unlock treatments for diseases currently considered incurable.

In artificial intelligence, quantum computing could accelerate machine learning algorithms by optimizing large datasets more efficiently. Quantum-enhanced AI systems might learn faster, generalize better, and uncover patterns that are invisible to classical approaches. This synergy — where AI aids quantum development and vice versa — is referred to as the quantum-AI nexus, and it promises a radical leap in capabilities.

Transition from Classical to Quantum Algorithms

The transition from classical to quantum computing is not simply about swapping hardware — it requires an entirely new approach to software design and problem-solving. Most current algorithms are designed for deterministic, linear machines. Quantum algorithms, in contrast, often rely on probabilistic and non-linear logic.

Early examples of quantum algorithms include Shor's algorithm for factoring and Grover's algorithm for searching unsorted databases faster than any classical counterpart. These algorithms illustrate how quantum mechanics can reduce complexity from exponential to polynomial time, essentially transforming what was previously unsolvable into the solvable.

However, this transition is far from seamless. Quantum computers are currently plagued by decoherence, where qubits lose their quantum state due to environmental interference, and error rates that are far higher than in classical systems. This has led to the development of quantum error correction techniques, which require even more qubits and advanced control systems. As a result, the practical realization of quantum computing remains in the realm of Noisy Intermediate-Scale Quantum (NISQ) devices — machines that are powerful but not yet universally applicable.

Developers must also rethink programming paradigms. Languages like Qiskit (by IBM), Cirq (by Google), and Quipper are being used to explore quantum software development, but these are still in their infancy. New logic structures, debugging tools, and training frameworks will be needed to make quantum computing accessible to a wider audience.

Implications for Security and Privacy

One of the most significant and controversial consequences of quantum computing is its impact on digital security and privacy. As mentioned, modern encryption standards — including RSA, ECC (Elliptic Curve Cryptography), and even blockchain technologies — are vulnerable to quantum attacks. The threat is not just theoretical. Intelligence agencies around the world are believed to be harvesting encrypted data now, anticipating that they will be able to decrypt it in the future when quantum capabilities mature.

This leads to a concept called "harvest now, decrypt later," which poses immense risks to personal privacy, national security, and intellectual property. Organizations must begin transitioning to quantum-resistant encryption protocols — such as lattice-based, hash-based, and code-based cryptography — even before quantum computers are fully operational.

At the same time, quantum technology offers new forms of security. Quantum key distribution (QKD) allows two parties to generate a shared, secret key that is theoretically immune to eavesdropping. Any attempt to observe the key alters its state, making the interception detectable. Countries like China and the U.S. are already experimenting with quantum-secured communication satellites and fibre-optic networks.

The paradox is stark: quantum computing could both destroy and rebuild digital security frameworks. Societies must decide whether to embrace this duality by designing flexible, adaptive security systems — or risk being blindsided by the very tools they helped create.

The Road Ahead: Promise and Peril

As of now, companies like Google, IBM, Rigetti, and D-Wave are pioneering the path toward commercial quantum computing. In 2019, Google claimed to have achieved quantum supremacy — performing a calculation in 200 seconds that would take a classical supercomputer 10,000 years. While contested, this milestone hints at the potential scale of change ahead.

Despite the hype, general-purpose quantum computers remain years — if not decades — away. The field is still grappling with foundational issues such as scalability, coherence times, and error correction. But the direction is clear: we are moving toward a future where quantum computing is not just a scientific curiosity but a transformative technology.

This transformation raises deep ethical and philosophical questions. Who controls quantum access? How do we ensure equity in the quantum era? Will quantum breakthroughs reinforce existing power structures or democratize technology? The answers remain uncertain, but they are urgent.

The Age of Quantum Computing is not just another chapter in the technological revolution — it is a paradigm shift. With its power to solve problems previously deemed impossible, quantum computing could redefine science, society, and the structure of knowledge itself. But this same power, left unchecked, could also fracture the systems we rely on. As we stand on the threshold of this new era, the challenge is not just to build quantum machines but to align them with human values, social good, and collective responsibility.

Chapter 5: Virtual Reality: Escaping or Enhancing Reality?

The idea of stepping into another world—a fully immersive, three-dimensional space where the laws of physics can be bent, environments altered at will, and identities reimagined—was once the domain of science fiction. Today, virtual reality (VR) is no longer fantasy. It is a fast-evolving technology with increasing influence across a wide array of human experience, from how we play and learn to how we heal and socialize. But with its growing presence comes a crucial question: Is virtual reality a tool to enhance life, or a digital escape route from it?

The Evolution of VR and Its Applications

Virtual reality has roots that stretch back further than many realize. Early attempts in the 1960s, like Morton Heilig's Sensorama, aimed to simulate multisensory experiences through mechanical means. The 1980s saw the term "virtual reality" popularized alongside primitive head-mounted displays (HMDs) and glove input devices, but it wasn't until the 2010s—with the rise of affordable computing power and companies like Oculus, HTC, and Sony—that VR truly began to find its feet.

Modern VR technology typically involves a headset with stereoscopic displays, motion tracking, and increasingly sophisticated haptics. As hardware becomes more affordable and content more diverse, VR is expanding far beyond gaming. Medical students can now practice complex procedures in virtual simulations. Architects and engineers walk through buildings before laying a single brick. Artists sculpt in 3D space. Therapists treat phobias with controlled exposure scenarios. These are not novelty applications—they are real-world implementations changing the way we think, create, and engage with reality.

VR in Entertainment, Education, and Therapy

In entertainment, VR has revolutionized interactivity. Gaming, the most mature VR sector, provides immersive environments where users aren't just observers but active participants. The popularity of titles like *Beat Saber*, *Half-Life: Alyx*, and social spaces like *VRChat* demonstrate the appeal of engaging with content in a way that feels physically present.

Film and storytelling also evolve in VR, offering 360-degree narratives and interactive plots. Viewers are placed *inside* the story rather than simply watching it unfold. This opens the door for empathy-driven storytelling, where users can experience perspectives they'd never encounter in daily life—such as walking in the shoes of a refugee, or experiencing a day with a cognitive disorder.

In education, VR breaks down traditional limitations. Instead of reading about the Roman Empire, students can walk its streets. Complex concepts in physics, biology, or chemistry become visual and interactive, helping abstract ideas become concrete. Remote learners gain access to laboratories, field trips, and collaborative projects, all within virtual space.

Therapeutically, VR is emerging as a powerful tool. It is used to treat PTSD in veterans, anxiety disorders through controlled exposure, and even chronic pain via distraction therapy. Virtual environments provide safe spaces for trauma victims to confront and reframe past experiences under professional supervision. For neurodivergent individuals, VR can simulate social interactions, offering a controlled setting to build skills and confidence.

Risks of Escapism and Societal Detachment

Despite its many benefits, VR poses risks—chief among them the lure of escapism. In virtual worlds, people can become anyone, go anywhere, and exert control rarely found in real life. For some, this can be therapeutic. But for others, it becomes a substitute for real-world engagement. The danger lies in prolonged detachment.

The phenomenon is already manifesting. Cases of people preferring their virtual personas to their real ones, neglecting responsibilities, or forming relationships that exist solely in virtual space, are increasing. When the digital world offers more gratification, control, and connection than reality, the temptation to withdraw grows.

This isn't new. Television, video games, and the internet have all presented similar dilemmas. But VR amplifies the sense of presence, and thus the potential for psychological immersion. The consequences are more intense. Addiction, social isolation, and a deterioration of physical health due to sedentary behaviour are serious concerns.

Moreover, virtual spaces often lack regulation. Harassment, identity manipulation, and inappropriate content are prevalent, particularly in social VR platforms. Without effective moderation, users—especially minors—can be exposed to harmful interactions, reinforcing trauma or creating new mental health challenges.

Balancing Immersion with Reality

The challenge, then, is balance. VR's strength lies in its ability to blur the lines between reality and simulation—but it's also a potential weakness. As the technology matures, society must develop strategies to ensure its use enhances rather than replaces real life.

One approach is integration rather than substitution. For example, rather than replacing classroom time with VR, educators can use it to complement lessons. In therapy, VR should not be a standalone tool but part of a broader treatment strategy. In entertainment, time limits and content awareness can help manage engagement and avoid compulsive use.

Tech developers have a role to play, too. Design ethics should prioritize user well-being. This includes implementing reminders for breaks, fostering inclusive community standards, and building in accessibility for people with physical or cognitive disabilities. Transparency in data collection and user privacy must be central—many current systems quietly track eye movement, emotional responses, and spatial behaviour.

There's also a societal responsibility. Discussions around the use of VR need to happen not just in academic or developer spaces but among parents, educators, healthcare providers, and legislators. Establishing norms early can guide responsible use before problematic habits become entrenched.

Philosophical Implications of Virtual Realities

Beyond practical concerns, VR raises deep philosophical questions. If one can experience joy, connection, and purpose in a virtual space, is that experience any less real? Does it matter whether our meaningful moments happen in simulated environments if our minds interpret them as genuine?

This line of thinking invites comparisons to debates about consciousness and reality itself. If reality is constructed in the brain—through sensory input and cognitive processing—then virtual experiences can be seen as just another version of "real." However, the problem arises when those experiences replace opportunities for real-world growth, learning, and community.

And yet, there may come a time when the distinction between digital and physical becomes irrelevant. As neural interfaces improve and our ability to create hyper-realistic simulations grows, we may not even be able to tell the difference. Would it matter if a friendship began in the physical world or a virtual café? Would love, grief, and triumph feel any less intense in a digital construct?

These questions aren't meant to justify escapism but to highlight the complexity of the path we're on. VR has the potential to enrich lives—but also to confuse the boundaries of those lives.

The Road Ahead

The trajectory of VR is clear: it will become more immersive, more accessible, and more deeply integrated into everyday life. What remains uncertain is how we will choose to engage with it. Will it be a mirror to better understand ourselves? A canvas for creativity and connection? Or a veil to hide behind when reality feels too raw?

Ultimately, the power of VR lies not just in the technology itself, but in how we choose to wield it. It is neither inherently good nor bad—it is a tool, a mirror, and a potential world of its own. Whether it leads us closer to understanding ourselves or further away from the essence of human connection depends on the boundaries we set, the values we uphold, and the realities we choose to build—both virtual and otherwise.

Chapter 6: The Internet of Things: A Fully Connected World

In a world increasingly defined by interconnectivity, the Internet of Things (IoT) has emerged as a transformative force. From smart homes to industrial automation, IoT is reshaping how we live, work, and interact with our environment. At its core, IoT refers to a network of physical devices embedded with sensors, software, and other technologies, all connected to the internet to collect and exchange data. But beyond the buzzwords, what does a fully connected world truly mean, and what are the benefits and risks of living within one?

Definition and Scope of IoT

The Internet of Things encompasses a vast and rapidly expanding network of devices. These range from everyday household items—thermostats, refrigerators, light bulbs—to advanced industrial machinery, urban infrastructure, and wearable health monitors. Anything that can be equipped with sensors and a means of communication can be part of the IoT ecosystem.

This network allows devices to talk to one another, share information in real time, and respond autonomously to changing conditions. For example, a smart irrigation system in agriculture can detect soil moisture levels and adjust water usage without human intervention. In a smart city, traffic lights can coordinate with each other to optimize traffic flow. These scenarios showcase IoT's core promise: a more responsive, efficient, and intelligent world.

The scope of IoT continues to grow with the proliferation of 5G networks, edge computing, and cheaper sensors. As billions of devices come online, the vision of an always-connected, intelligent environment becomes increasingly feasible. But with this scale comes complexity—and consequences.

Benefits: Improved Efficiency, Convenience, Data Collection

One of the most significant advantages of IoT is the potential for improved efficiency across sectors. In manufacturing, predictive maintenance powered by IoT sensors can identify equipment issues before they lead to downtime. Energy systems can optimize power usage dynamically, reducing waste and lowering costs. In logistics, GPS-enabled IoT devices can track shipments in real-time, allowing companies to streamline operations and reduce delivery times.

For consumers, IoT translates to convenience. Smart homes allow for automation of lighting, heating, and security systems. Voice-controlled assistants can manage daily tasks. Wearable devices track health metrics, helping individuals monitor their well-being and even alerting users to potential medical issues before they become serious.

Perhaps most valuable is the data generated by these devices. IoT offers a new layer of insight into behaviour, environment, and system performance. Cities can analyse traffic patterns to reduce congestion. Hospitals can monitor patient vitals remotely. Businesses can understand customer preferences with unprecedented granularity.

This data-driven approach opens the door to innovation and personalization. Services can adapt in real-time to users' needs. Systems can self-optimize. The promise is clear: smarter environments that work seamlessly in the background to improve quality of life.

Privacy Concerns with Pervasive Connectivity

However, the same data that fuels these benefits also introduces serious privacy concerns. As more aspects of our lives become digitized and monitored, the potential for surveillance—by corporations, governments, or malicious actors—increases.

IoT devices often collect highly personal information: location, voice recordings, health data, daily routines. This data can be used to create detailed profiles of individuals, sometimes without their informed consent. Worse, many devices are not transparent about what they collect or how they use the information.

Data breaches involving IoT devices have already occurred, exposing sensitive information. The problem is compounded by the fact that many devices lack robust security measures. Unlike traditional computers or smartphones, IoT devices often have limited processing power, making it difficult to implement strong encryption or regular software updates.

This raises ethical questions about consent, data ownership, and surveillance. Should a smart TV be allowed to listen in on conversations? Can a fitness tracker sell health data to third parties? In a connected world, these questions are not abstract—they are immediate and unresolved.

The Challenge of Security in an Interconnected World

Security is one of the most pressing challenges facing the IoT landscape. With billions of devices connected to the internet, each one becomes a potential point of vulnerability. Hackers can exploit these weak links to gain access to broader networks, as seen in large-scale cyberattacks like the Mirai botnet, which hijacked IoT devices to launch distributed denial-of-service (DDoS) attacks.

The diversity of devices and lack of standardization exacerbate the issue. Manufacturers often prioritize cost and speed to market over security. Devices may ship with default passwords, outdated software, or unpatched vulnerabilities. Once installed, users are rarely prompted to update firmware or adjust security settings.

The consequences of insecure IoT networks are not just digital—they can be physical. Imagine a hacked pacemaker, a compromised car, or a disabled home security system. As IoT becomes embedded in critical infrastructure, the stakes grow higher.

Solutions exist, but they require coordination. Industry standards must be enforced to ensure baseline security measures. Governments can play a role in regulation and oversight. Consumers need greater awareness and education. And developers must build security into design from the start, not as an afterthought.

Moreover, there is a need for better lifecycle management of IoT devices. Many are deployed and then forgotten, with little support for updates or secure decommissioning. This long tail of neglected devices creates a growing risk over time.

Looking Ahead: Managing the Trade-offs

The Internet of Things is not inherently good or bad—it is a reflection of how we choose to implement it. The benefits are substantial, but so are the risks. Striking the right balance requires conscious choices at every level: design, policy, and personal use.

As IoT continues to evolve, we must ask difficult questions. How do we ensure equitable access to the benefits of connectivity without creating surveillance societies? What responsibilities do companies have in safeguarding user data? Where do we draw the line between convenience and intrusion?

Ultimately, a fully connected world will challenge our assumptions about privacy, control, and autonomy. But it also offers a powerful opportunity: to create environments that adapt, learn, and respond in ways that enhance human potential. The key is to remain vigilant, informed, and proactive in shaping the future of IoT—before it shapes us without our consent.

In the grand narrative of human progress, few advancements rival the profound potential of biotechnology. The ability to manipulate the very fabric of life — DNA — signifies a seismic shift in how we understand disease, heredity, evolution, and even identity. We are now in an era where genetic engineering, once confined to science fiction, has become a scientific reality. At the heart of this revolution are technologies like CRISPR-Cas9, gene therapy, synthetic biology, and genome sequencing, each opening up new frontiers that could redefine the limits of medicine, biology, and humanity itself.

Advances in Genetic Engineering

CRISPR-Cas9 (Clustered Regularly Interspaced Short Palindromic Repeats) is arguably the most transformative biotechnology of the 21st century. This gene-editing tool allows scientists to cut and modify DNA with unprecedented precision. Unlike earlier, less predictable methods, CRISPR enables targeted edits, offering the potential to correct genetic defects, remove disease-causing mutations, and even insert new, beneficial traits.

The development of CRISPR has already yielded remarkable results. Researchers have used it to treat sickle cell anaemia, muscular dystrophy, and certain forms of hereditary blindness in clinical trials. In agriculture, CRISPR has been used to produce crops that are more resistant to drought, pests, and disease — all without introducing foreign DNA, a distinction that sidesteps many concerns related to traditional genetically modified organisms (GMOs).

Gene therapy, another critical arm of biotechnology, involves inserting healthy copies of genes into a patient's cells to replace faulty or missing ones. After decades of slow progress and setbacks, gene therapy is finally becoming a mainstream treatment option. Conditions once considered untreatable — such as spinal muscular atrophy and some types of inherited blindness — are now being addressed with gene-based therapies. Some treatments offer not just symptom relief but the possibility of a cure.

Beyond CRISPR and gene therapy, the mapping of the human genome has set the stage for a wave of personalized medicine. With the cost of genome sequencing dropping dramatically, individuals can now receive treatments tailored to their genetic profiles. This means more effective drugs, fewer side effects, and new possibilities for prevention.

Potential for Curing Diseases and Enhancing Human Traits

Biotechnology holds immense promise in the realm of disease eradication. From cancer to cystic fibrosis, from HIV to rare genetic disorders, the potential for permanent cures is becoming more tangible. CRISPR has even been used to edit the genes of embryos to eliminate inherited diseases, a deeply controversial but scientifically feasible act.

But the same tools used to cure can also be used to enhance. This introduces a new and largely unexplored domain of human augmentation. What if we could eliminate the genes responsible for depression, addiction, or aging? What if we could enhance memory, physical endurance, or intelligence through genetic editing?

These questions shift biotechnology from a medical discipline into a philosophical and ethical battleground. The line between therapy and enhancement is blurry, and as techniques improve, the demand for "designer traits" may increase. Parents might seek genetic alterations for their children to improve height, eye colour, or athletic ability. This opens the door to a form of eugenics by choice, raising difficult questions about equity, diversity, and identity.

The potential benefits are staggering, but so are the consequences. Unequal access to enhancement technologies could lead to a new class divide: those with engineered advantages and those without. The human genome could become another site of inequality, with social, economic, and ethical dimensions that are difficult to predict and harder to manage.

Ethical Implications of "Playing God"

Manipulating the genome carries a heavy ethical burden. The phrase "playing God" has echoed through debates on cloning, stem cell research, and now gene editing. But it's not just a rhetorical question — it's a genuine concern about where the boundaries of human intervention should lie.

On one side, proponents argue that the moral imperative is clear: if we have the power to eliminate suffering, we are obligated to use it. They see biotechnology as a tool of compassion, a means to end disease and improve quality of life. On the other side, critics warn of unintended consequences, both biological and societal. Genes rarely act in isolation; changing one could have ripple effects throughout the genome and across generations.

The case of He Jiankui, the Chinese scientist who used CRISPR to alter the genomes of twin girls in 2018, illustrates the ethical minefield. His experiment was widely condemned by the global scientific community for violating ethical standards and exposing the children to unknown risks. It also revealed how quickly scientific capability can outpace regulation and oversight.

Religious and philosophical perspectives add further layers to the debate. Some argue that altering the human genome disrupts a divine order or the natural course of evolution. Others see it as an extension of humanity's long-standing pursuit of health and longevity. There is no consensus, and perhaps there never will be. But the speed of biotechnological progress demands a level of ethical vigilance that can match its scientific ambition.

The Division Between Natural and Modified Life Forms

As biotechnology reshapes life at a fundamental level, the definition of what is "natural" becomes increasingly ambiguous. When a child is born with edited genes, is that child still a product of nature? When organisms are created from scratch using synthetic biology, are they alive in the traditional sense, or something entirely new?

The boundary between natural and artificial blurs further with the advent of synthetic genomes. Scientists have already created synthetic bacteria with reduced genomes, stripped down to the bare essentials for life. These minimal cells are not just curiosities; they serve as platforms for manufacturing pharmaceuticals, biofuels, and other valuable compounds.

Even more radical is the possibility of creating entirely new life forms with no evolutionary precedent. This is no longer speculation. Researchers are exploring the design of organisms with novel genetic codes that include synthetic amino acids, offering properties unknown in the natural world.

These developments challenge existing biological classifications. They also raise practical concerns about containment, mutation, and unintended ecological consequences. Modified organisms could potentially outcompete natural ones or disrupt ecosystems in ways we can't fully anticipate.

Society will need to grapple with these questions. Will there be legal distinctions between natural and modified life forms? Will people with genetically enhanced traits be considered fundamentally different? How do we ensure that biotechnological innovations do not lead to a new form of discrimination or biological hierarchy?

Looking Forward: Responsibility and Regulation

The future of biotechnology is not just about what can be done, but what should be done. It is a future that must be shaped by a multidisciplinary approach, bringing together scientists, ethicists, policymakers, and the public.

Strong international frameworks will be essential. Biotechnology does not respect national borders, and decisions made in one country can have global consequences. Oversight must be agile enough to keep pace with innovation while ensuring safety, equity, and ethical integrity.

Public understanding is equally important. As biotechnology becomes more visible and impactful, transparent communication will be vital. People must be informed participants in the debate, not passive recipients of its outcomes. Education, public dialogue, and accessible science reporting will play a critical role in shaping opinion and policy.

Ultimately, biotechnology gives us a kind of authorship over life. But with that power comes the responsibility to write wisely. The code of life is not just a biological sequence; it is a narrative of what it means to be human. As we edit, enhance, and evolve, we must do so with care, humility, and a deep respect for the complexity of life itself.

Chapter 8: Space Exploration: Humanity's New Frontier

Space exploration has always fascinated human imagination. From Galileo's first telescope to the Apollo moon landings, and now to the robotic missions on Mars and plans for lunar bases, humanity has been steadily pushing the boundaries of what is possible. But in the 21st century, space is no longer just a scientific pursuit; it is quickly becoming a strategic frontier for survival, resource acquisition, and perhaps even a new beginning.

Current Achievements in Space Travel

Over the past two decades, space travel has entered a new phase driven by a combination of public and private initiatives. NASA, the European Space Agency (ESA), China National Space Administration (CNSA), and private companies like SpaceX, Blue Origin, and Rocket Lab are achieving milestones that were once the stuff of science fiction.

Mars missions, both robotic and conceptual, represent a central focus. NASA's Perseverance rover has been exploring Mars since 2021, searching for signs of ancient life and collecting samples for potential return to Earth. China's Tianwen-1 has successfully landed its Zhurong rover, making China the second country to land and operate a rover on Mars. These missions provide critical data not just for scientific purposes but also for future human colonization.

Meanwhile, the Artemis program aims to establish a permanent human presence on the Moon by the 2030s. NASA plans to build the Lunar Gateway, an orbiting outpost that will facilitate missions to and from the lunar surface. The idea is not just to revisit the Moon, but to use it as a stepping stone for Mars and beyond.

Private enterprise has introduced competition and innovation. SpaceX has developed reusable rockets, significantly reducing the cost of space travel. Its Starship vehicle is being tested for deep-space missions, with aspirations to ferry humans to Mars. These developments suggest that space travel is transitioning from experimental to operational, making extraterrestrial life more than a distant dream.

The Potential for Extraterrestrial Colonization

The idea of establishing human settlements beyond Earth is no longer confined to speculative fiction. Plans are being drawn up for colonies on the Moon and Mars, with habitats designed to sustain life in harsh conditions. The rationale for such colonization is multifaceted.

First, it offers a form of existential insurance. Earth is vulnerable to natural disasters, pandemics, climate change, and even nuclear war. Establishing a human presence on other celestial bodies could ensure the survival of our species in the event of catastrophe.

Second, colonization can drive technological and biological innovations. Adapting to space environments requires advancements in sustainable agriculture, closed-loop life support systems, and possibly genetic enhancements to cope with radiation and low gravity. These innovations could have applications on Earth, especially in areas facing climate-related stress.

Third, extraterrestrial colonization could transform our cultural and philosophical understanding of humanity. Living on another planet would require a shift in identity, ethics, and governance. It might force us to rethink concepts like nationality, citizenship, and ecological responsibility. A Mars colony could serve as a laboratory for new forms of society, perhaps more egalitarian or cooperative than those on Earth.

However, the challenges are formidable. Mars, for example, has a thin atmosphere, extreme temperatures, and no magnetic field to shield against radiation. Establishing self-sufficient colonies will require a level of engineering and resilience that humanity has never before demonstrated. But the pursuit itself pushes the boundaries of what we are capable of achieving.

Resource Utilization in Space

One of the key drivers behind space exploration is the potential for resource extraction. Space is rich in materials that are rare or diminishing on Earth. Asteroids contain vast quantities of platinum-group metals, water ice, and other valuable minerals.

Companies like Planetary Resources and Deep Space Industries were early pioneers in asteroid mining concepts, although they faced financial and technical challenges. More recently, space agencies have begun studying the feasibility of extracting resources from the Moon and near-Earth asteroids.

Water ice found at the lunar poles could be converted into oxygen and hydrogen, providing both breathable air and rocket fuel. This would make the Moon an important refuelling station for deeper space missions.

Mining in space could also reduce the environmental strain on Earth. Instead of digging deeper and polluting more, humanity could look outward. However, this raises legal and ethical concerns. The Outer Space Treaty of 1967 prohibits national appropriation of celestial bodies, but it is vague about commercial exploitation. New frameworks will be needed to regulate ownership, environmental protection, and equitable distribution of space-derived wealth.

Philosophical Implications of Life Beyond Earth

Beyond the practical and scientific aspects, space exploration carries profound philosophical weight. The search for extraterrestrial life, whether microbial or intelligent, challenges our assumptions about uniqueness and purpose.

If we find even a single microbe on Mars or a distant exoplanet, it would suggest that life is not a fluke confined to Earth. It would imply that the universe is teeming with biological possibilities, forcing us to reconsider our place in the cosmos. This could have enormous implications for religion, philosophy, and ethics.

Moreover, the act of exploring and settling new worlds invites introspection. What values should we carry into space? How do we avoid repeating the colonial and exploitative mistakes of Earth's history? If we become a multi-planetary species, do we redefine what it means to be human?

Space also offers a kind of psychological mirror. As astronauts have often reported, seeing Earth from orbit produces the "Overview Effect" — a cognitive shift that fosters a sense of unity, fragility, and interconnectedness. It is possible that expanding our perspective to include other worlds could foster more humility and stewardship back home.

The Road Ahead

Space is vast, hostile, and indifferent to human life. But it is also full of opportunity. As we move further into this new frontier, we must balance ambition with caution, innovation with ethics, and exploration with reflection. The decisions we make in the coming decades will not only shape our future in space but also redefine our legacy on Earth.

The stars are no longer out of reach. But the question remains: what kind of explorers will we choose to be?

Chapter 9: Renewable Energy: A Sustainable Future

The 21st century is defined by a paradox. On one hand, we've reached unprecedented levels of technological progress and global connectivity. On the other, we face the escalating consequences of our long-standing dependence on fossil fuels — rising temperatures, extreme weather, vanishing ecosystems, and deepening inequalities. Against this backdrop, the transition to renewable energy stands not just as a solution, but as a necessity. It is the axis around which the future of human civilization may turn — for better or worse.

This chapter unpacks the core drivers, challenges, and opportunities of the global energy transition. From the roots of fossil fuel dependency to the frontiers of solar innovation and battery storage, we explore how renewable energy is reshaping economies, addressing climate instability, and reimagining the role of power — literally and politically — in human society.

Transition from Fossil Fuels to Renewable Sources

The story of fossil fuels is a story of momentum — economic, industrial, and political. Since the Industrial Revolution, coal, oil, and natural gas have formed the backbone of global energy systems. Their abundance and energy density helped fuel massive industrial expansion, power grids, vehicles, and economies. But this progress came at a cost: emissions, pollution, and ecological breakdown. The science is now indisputable. If we continue on a fossil-fuelled path, the consequences will be irreversible.

Global emissions from fossil fuels were nearly 37 billion tonnes of CO_2 in 2022. The energy sector alone accounts for about three-quarters of global greenhouse gas emissions. Continuing this trajectory undermines any hope of limiting global warming to 1.5°C or even 2°C above pre-industrial levels — thresholds that climate scientists identify as tipping points.

Recognizing this, governments, businesses, and civil society are beginning to pivot. Coal plants are being decommissioned. Oil exploration licenses are increasingly challenged. And international agreements like the Paris Accord have formalized carbon reduction commitments, even if progress remains uneven.

But transitioning to renewable energy isn't just about unplugging one system and plugging in another. It involves redesigning infrastructure from the ground up — updating transmission lines, rethinking energy storage, re-training workers, and redefining energy markets. It requires replacing centralized, fossil-fuel-driven grids with more flexible, decentralized systems powered by sun, wind, water, and biomass. And most critically, it requires the political will to stand up to entrenched industries that profit from the status quo.

Still, despite resistance, the direction is clear: renewables are now the fastest-growing segment of the global energy mix. In 2023, over 80% of all new electricity capacity added worldwide came from renewable sources, with solar and wind leading the charge.

Innovations in Solar, Wind, and Battery Technology

One of the most encouraging aspects of the energy transition is the pace of technological innovation. Over the past two decades, clean energy has gone from niche to mainstream — driven largely by improvements in technology, scale, and affordability.

Solar Energy

Once considered prohibitively expensive, solar photovoltaic (PV) systems are now among the cheapest sources of electricity in history. The cost of solar power has fallen by more than 85% since 2010, thanks to improvements in panel efficiency, manufacturing processes, and global supply chains.

Modern solar panels convert sunlight to electricity at rates that would've seemed impossible just a few years ago. Bifacial panels can absorb light from both sides. Thin-film technologies offer lightweight, flexible alternatives for unusual surfaces. And perovskite-based solar cells — still in development — promise even higher efficiencies with lower production costs.

Beyond land-based panels, innovations like floating solar farms are gaining ground. These systems sit on reservoirs or lakes, minimizing land use while reducing evaporation and improving energy output through natural cooling. Solar windows and building-integrated photovoltaics (BIPV) are also becoming more viable, turning urban infrastructure into power-generating assets.

Wind Energy

Wind power has experienced a parallel boom, especially in regions with consistent wind patterns. Like solar, the cost of wind energy has dropped dramatically — over 70% in the last 10 years — making it one of the most competitive sources of new electricity.

Modern wind turbines are technological marvels. Taller than ever before and equipped with AI-based sensors, they maximize power output by adjusting blade angles in real-time. Offshore wind is particularly promising. With fewer land-use constraints and stronger, more consistent winds, offshore farms can generate massive amounts of power. The UK and Denmark already rely on offshore wind for a significant portion of their electricity, and other coastal nations are quickly following suit.

Floating wind farms — still in early deployment — allow turbines to be installed in deeper waters, opening up vast new areas for development. These are tethered to the ocean floor and use advanced mooring systems and stabilizing technologies.

Battery Storage

Renewables are intermittent. The sun doesn't shine at night, and the wind doesn't always blow. Without effective storage, this variability can cause supply issues. That's where battery technology comes in.

Lithium-ion batteries currently dominate the market, and their performance continues to improve. Energy density is increasing. Charging times are decreasing. And prices have dropped by more than 85% since 2010. Tesla's Powerwall, and similar home or industrial-scale systems, allow solar energy to be stored during the day and used at night.

But the innovation isn't stopping with lithium. Solid-state batteries, with higher energy capacity and reduced fire risk, are moving from lab to prototype. Flow batteries, which store energy in tanks of liquid electrolyte, offer scalable storage with longer lifespans. And grid-scale battery systems, like the Hornsdale Power Reserve in South Australia, are already proving they can stabilize entire regions in real time.

Alternative storage methods are also gaining attention: pumped hydro, compressed air, molten salt, and even gravity-based systems are part of the evolving landscape.

Together, these technologies are closing the reliability gap, turning renewables from variable to dependable — a game-changer for widespread adoption.

Addressing Climate Change and Resource Scarcity

Transitioning to renewable energy isn't just about cleaner power. It's about rethinking our relationship with the planet and its finite resources.

The link between fossil fuels and climate change is well-established. Combustion of oil, coal, and gas releases CO_2, methane, and other greenhouse gases into the atmosphere. These trap heat, disrupt weather patterns, melt glaciers, and acidify oceans. Renewable energy breaks this chain. Solar, wind, hydro, and geothermal systems emit little to no greenhouse gases during operation.

In practical terms, replacing a single coal plant with a solar farm can prevent millions of tonnes of CO_2 emissions each year. When scaled globally, the potential for climate mitigation is massive.

But beyond emissions, renewables also offer a reprieve from resource depletion. Fossil fuels are finite. Extracting them requires destructive methods — mining, drilling, fracking — that scar landscapes and pollute ecosystems. In contrast, solar and wind are effectively infinite. They don't require extraction. They don't run out. And they don't poison the air or water.

They also use significantly less water. Thermal power plants — coal, nuclear, and natural gas — consume vast amounts of water for cooling. In drought-prone areas, this exacerbates scarcity. Solar PV and wind turbines require almost no water, offering a low-impact solution.

And as materials science advances, even the resource inputs of renewable systems — rare earth metals, lithium, cobalt — are being optimized. Closed-loop recycling systems, ethical sourcing frameworks, and new chemistries are reducing dependence on unsustainable mining practices.

Economic and Social Impact of the Energy Transition

The economic implications of the renewable energy transition are enormous — and mostly positive. Far from being a burden, the transition presents one of the largest job-creation opportunities in human history.

According to the International Renewable Energy Agency (IRENA), the global renewable energy sector employed over 13 million people in 2022, with projections suggesting that number could rise to 38 million by 2030. These jobs span a wide spectrum: manufacturing, installation, operations, maintenance, research, and policymaking.

Countries investing in renewables are not just cleaning their grids — they're revitalizing economies. Solar panel manufacturing in Vietnam, wind turbine engineering in Denmark, battery production in South Korea — these industries are becoming pillars of national economic strategy.

Energy Access and Equity

Renewables are also expanding access to power in underserved regions. In parts of Sub-Saharan Africa and South Asia, centralized grids are patchy or non-existent. Decentralized solar microgrids offer a faster, cheaper, and more resilient alternative. They enable remote communities to power homes, schools, clinics, and businesses — lifting people out of energy poverty.

Importantly, these systems can be locally owned and managed, democratizing energy ownership and reducing dependence on large utilities or foreign fuel imports.

Social Justice and Inclusion

But the transition must be just. Coal miners and oil workers cannot be left behind. Retraining, community reinvestment, and transitional support are essential. Otherwise, backlash and inequality will grow, undermining climate efforts.

It's also vital to ensure that clean energy supply chains are not exploitative. The mining of cobalt in the Congo, or lithium in South America, must be monitored for human rights and environmental abuses. Sustainable energy must be sustainable in every sense — including social and ethical dimensions.

Chapter 10: Smart Cities: The Urban Revolution

Cities have always been centres of progress. From the bustling trade routes of ancient Mesopotamia to the towering skylines of today's metropolises, urban environments reflect the priorities, technologies, and tensions of their time. Now, as we stand on the threshold of a new era defined by connectivity, automation, and data, cities are once again evolving — becoming not just more advanced, but more *intelligent*.

The term "smart city" has been thrown around enough to feel like a buzzword, but beneath the hype lies a real transformation. These cities are wired — literally and digitally — to respond to human needs more dynamically. They aim to integrate information and communication technology (ICT) with urban infrastructure to improve efficiency, sustainability, and quality of life. But this evolution isn't without its risks. As cities collect more data, track more behaviours, and automate more systems, questions about surveillance, control, and inequality become harder to ignore.

In this chapter, we'll unpack what smart cities really are — not in abstract ideals, but in concrete systems and real-world applications. We'll look at the benefits they offer, the threats they pose, and which cities are already building the urban future.

What is a Smart City?

At its core, a smart city uses technology to make everyday urban life function better — more efficiently, more sustainably, and ideally, more humanely. But this isn't just about apps or fast internet. It's about deeply integrating digital systems into the physical environment: sensors embedded in roads, AI managing traffic flow, data platforms coordinating waste collection, and citizens engaging with city services through interactive platforms.

There isn't a single definition of a smart city because the concept shifts depending on context. A city in a developing region might focus on smart energy and clean water. A European capital might prioritize congestion management, housing efficiency, or participatory digital governance.

Still, there are common components that most smart cities share:

1. Data Infrastructure

This is the nervous system of any smart city. It includes IoT (Internet of Things) sensors, connected devices, cloud storage, and AI-based data analytics. These systems constantly gather and process data from every corner of the city — from traffic lights and trash bins to air quality monitors and utility meters.

2. Mobility and Transportation

Smart traffic lights adjust to real-time congestion. Autonomous buses and e-scooter fleets reduce reliance on private cars. Integrated public transport apps show real-time arrivals, recommend efficient routes, and let users pay digitally across modes.

3. Energy and Utilities

Smart grids balance electricity supply and demand dynamically, incorporating renewable sources like solar and wind. Smart meters let residents track their consumption. LED street lighting dims or brightens based on pedestrian movement or time of day.

4. Buildings and Infrastructure

Smart buildings adjust heating, lighting, and air flow based on occupancy. Maintenance systems can predict equipment failures before they happen. Green roofs and materials reduce urban heat and energy costs.

5. Governance and Citizen Engagement

Digital platforms allow residents to report potholes, submit feedback, or participate in local decision-making. Chatbots answer municipal queries. Blockchain systems can increase transparency in budgeting and procurement.

6. Healthcare and Public Safety

Remote health-monitoring systems connect citizens with local clinics. Predictive policing software analyses crime data to allocate resources. Emergency systems trigger alerts based on real-time environmental or traffic data.

Together, these components form a dynamic, interconnected network. Ideally, each element reinforces the others, creating feedback loops that keep the city running smoothly and adapting continuously.

Benefits: Efficient Resource Management, Enhanced Living Conditions

When smart cities work well, their impact on everyday life is significant. The benefits aren't abstract — they're tangible improvements that touch energy, health, housing, safety, and overall quality of life.

1. Energy Efficiency and Sustainability

Smart systems reduce waste and improve sustainability. Take energy, for example. With smart grids, electricity isn't just distributed blindly. It's managed in real-time, routed where it's needed most, and stored when not. Buildings equipped with smart thermostats and occupancy sensors use far less power. Cities like Amsterdam and Barcelona have cut emissions substantially by modernizing how energy is consumed and distributed.

2. Mobility and Reduced Congestion

Traffic remains one of the most frustrating parts of urban life. Smart mobility systems help ease that. AI-powered traffic lights can cut commute times by 20–40% in some cities. Ride-sharing algorithms reduce empty car journeys. In Singapore, the government uses a city-wide sensor system to manage vehicle flows — adjusting tolls and rerouting traffic dynamically to minimize congestion.

3. Waste Management and Cleanliness

Smart bins equipped with sensors notify waste services when they're full. This reduces unnecessary trips and lowers emissions from garbage trucks. In Seoul, these systems have reduced city waste collection costs by up to 30%, while improving recycling rates.

4. Water Management

Cities like Los Angeles and Cape Town use smart water meters to detect leaks, reduce overuse, and forecast shortages. These tools are especially critical in drought-prone areas, where water mismanagement can quickly escalate into crisis.

5. Enhanced Public Safety

Integrated surveillance systems — while controversial — can help respond faster to emergencies. AI can detect unusual behaviour patterns and trigger alerts. During floods or fires, sensor data can automatically update evacuation routes or cut power in high-risk zones.

6. Digital Public Services

Long gone are the days of queuing at city hall for minor paperwork. In many smart cities, services have moved online: permits, fines, service requests, voting, all through a mobile device. Estonia, for instance, operates one of the most digitally advanced public systems, with over 99% of public services available online.

7. Social Inclusion and Citizen Participation

Digital platforms can democratize city planning. Residents can participate in budgeting decisions, vote on local projects, or flag issues in their neighbourhoods via apps. This kind of civic tech fosters transparency and strengthens the relationship between governments and the governed.

Risks: Surveillance, Inequality, and Data Abuse

The flip side of all this connectivity is control. The same technologies that optimise traffic or utilities can also be used to monitor behaviour, restrict freedom, and erode privacy. Smart cities don't just raise technical questions — they raise political ones.

1. Surveillance and Privacy

Many smart cities rely on vast networks of cameras, microphones, and sensors. While these are often justified as crime-prevention tools, they also enable constant surveillance. In China, some cities use facial recognition systems tied to social credit scores — where jaywalking, bad debt, or political dissent can result in punishments ranging from slower internet to travel bans.

The technology isn't limited to authoritarian regimes. Even democratic nations have experimented with facial recognition in public spaces, often with minimal oversight. Without strict regulation, data from smart cities could be used to profile, discriminate, or suppress.

2. Data Exploitation

Urban data is valuable — not just to governments, but to corporations. Private firms often partner with cities to run services or manage infrastructure. But who owns the data? Who profits from it? In many cases, data collected from public space is monetised without consent, or stored with little transparency.

If not handled properly, this creates a situation where public infrastructure serves private profit, and citizens become sources of behavioural data — tracked, sorted, and targeted.

3. Technological Inequality

Smart cities can deepen the divide between those who are digitally connected and those who are not. Low-income residents, the elderly, and marginalised communities may lack access to smartphones or digital literacy — effectively excluding them from new systems. When everything moves online, those left behind face a new form of urban exclusion.

Moreover, wealthier cities have the resources to implement cutting-edge technologies, while poorer municipalities struggle to fund even basic infrastructure. This creates a "two-speed" world of urban development — high-tech utopias for some, basic services for others.

4. System Failures and Cybersecurity

With increased reliance on digital infrastructure comes increased vulnerability. Hackers can disable traffic lights, disrupt power grids, or hijack surveillance networks. Without strong cybersecurity, smart cities become high-value targets for cyberattacks — not just from criminals, but from nation-states.

Cities Leading the Charge

While the concept of smart cities is global, some cities have emerged as leaders — either through technological innovation, sustainability, or governance models.

1. Barcelona, Spain

Barcelona has been a pioneer in using open data and citizen platforms. Its "Decidim" system lets residents vote on city projects, while smart streetlights and parking systems reduce emissions. The city's urban planning is people-focused, using "superblocks" to cut car use and return space to pedestrians.

2. Singapore

Singapore is one of the most advanced smart cities in the world. Its Smart Nation initiative integrates transport, healthcare, housing, and urban planning. Autonomous buses, cashless systems, real-time pollution monitoring, and smart elder care all operate within an efficient, tightly-managed framework.

3. Tallinn, Estonia

Estonia's capital is often held up as the gold standard of digital governance. Residents have digital IDs that let them access everything from healthcare to voting. Bureaucracy has been nearly eliminated. This digital backbone supports responsive, low-cost government with minimal red tape.

4. Seoul, South Korea

Seoul integrates public participation with high-tech infrastructure. It operates over 50,000 smart sensors and has an open data portal where developers can build citizen-focused apps. From smart waste bins to AI-assisted traffic, Seoul has set a high bar for urban efficiency.

5. Dubai, UAE

Dubai's Smart Dubai initiative aims to become the most data-driven city on the planet. Blockchain-backed identity systems, autonomous police units, and predictive maintenance tools are already deployed. While highly efficient, the city also raises questions about centralization and surveillance.

Education has always been a mirror of its time. In the agricultural age, it was basic and utilitarian. The industrial revolution reshaped it to serve factories and bureaucracies. Now, in the digital era, it is undergoing another transformation — one that is reshaping not just *what* we learn, but *how*, *when*, and *why* we learn. This chapter explores the evolving face of education in a world dominated by rapid technological change, AI-driven personalization, and increasing socio-digital divides.

The Rise of EdTech: From Chalkboards to Cloud-Based Classrooms

Technology has long been part of the classroom. Overhead projectors, televisions, and desktop computers were once at the frontier. But the last two decades have seen an explosion in education technology (edtech), from interactive whiteboards to full-scale online learning platforms.

Edtech is no longer just a supplementary tool. It's the backbone of many modern classrooms. Platforms like Google Classroom, Microsoft Teams, and Zoom became lifelines during the COVID-19 pandemic, proving how central digital tools had become. But beyond video conferencing, the landscape now includes:

- **Adaptive learning platforms** that adjust content difficulty in real time based on student performance
- **Gamified learning environments** that engage users through rewards, quests, and interactive narratives
- **Virtual and Augmented Reality** simulations that allow for immersive science labs or historical reconstructions
- **Learning Management Systems (LMS)** that track progress, automate assessments, and centralize content delivery

This isn't just modernization for its own sake. Properly implemented, these tools can enhance engagement, increase retention, and make learning more flexible.

Personalized Learning: AI as the New Tutor

One of the most significant breakthroughs in education is the use of AI to tailor learning experiences to the individual.

Traditional education often struggles with one-size-fits-all models. A single teacher might oversee 20 to 40 students, each with different strengths, weaknesses, and learning speeds. AI can help address this imbalance. Systems like Carnegie Learning and Squirrel AI in China analyse vast amounts of data to identify knowledge gaps, preferred learning styles, and even moments of cognitive fatigue.

The benefits of this personalization include:

- **Targeted Remediation**: AI can detect when a student doesn't understand a concept and offer different ways to explain it.

- **Pacing Adjustments**: Fast learners aren't held back, and struggling learners aren't left behind.

- **Motivational Tracking**: AI systems can pick up on engagement dips and adjust difficulty or content format accordingly.

- **Language Translation and Accessibility**: Tools powered by AI can instantly translate lessons or provide subtitles, opening education to a wider global audience.

However, AI in education isn't perfect. It lacks human intuition, emotional intelligence, and cultural nuance. There's also a risk of over-standardizing learning, where everything is reduced to metrics and gamified feedback loops. The role of the human teacher remains central, but increasingly they are becoming facilitators and mentors rather than information gatekeepers.

The Digital Divide: Not Everyone Gets a Seat at the Table

Despite the promises of edtech and AI, access remains a critical issue. Globally, around 2.7 billion people remain offline. Even in developed countries, digital divides persist along lines of income, geography, and ability.

Urban vs Rural: In many rural regions, internet access is unreliable or non-existent. Students may have limited access to devices, or rely on shared mobile phones.

Wealth Disparities: Wealthier families can afford better hardware, faster internet, and additional online tutoring services. Poorer families may lack even a quiet space for study.

Disability Access: Not all platforms are designed with accessibility in mind. Visually impaired students, for example, may struggle with poorly coded sites or platforms lacking screen reader compatibility.

Language and Localization: Many platforms are designed with English in mind, ignoring linguistic and cultural contexts elsewhere.

Bridging this gap is essential if the promise of Education 2.0 is to be equitable. Governments, NGOs, and tech firms have experimented with various solutions:

- Low-data versions of educational platforms
- Community Wi-Fi and mesh networks
- Distribution of low-cost devices like tablets or Chromebooks
- Open Educational Resources (OER) that provide free access to quality content

Still, the challenge is ongoing. Digital literacy itself is a barrier. Simply providing a laptop isn't enough if the user doesn't know how to navigate, assess information critically, or manage time online effectively.

Future Skills for a Tech-Driven World

As the education system transforms, so too must its goals. The traditional curriculum — often focused on rote memorization, standard testing, and outdated industrial-age knowledge — is becoming increasingly disconnected from the world students are entering.

The jobs of tomorrow demand different skill sets, many of which are not yet prioritized in mainstream schooling. Among the most important future-facing skills are:

1. Digital Literacy and Cybersecurity Awareness

It's no longer enough to know how to use a computer. Students need to understand digital privacy, recognize misinformation, and navigate online platforms responsibly.

2. Critical Thinking and Problem Solving

AI can retrieve facts, but interpreting them, applying logic, and evaluating evidence remain distinctly human strengths.

3. Creativity and Innovation

In a world where automation threatens routine jobs, creative and adaptive thinking will set individuals apart.

4. Emotional Intelligence and Collaboration

The future of work is deeply collaborative. Understanding group dynamics, empathy, and conflict resolution are vital.

5. Lifelong Learning and Self-Motivation

Technology will continue to evolve. Students must be equipped to continuously re-skill and adapt to new tools and environments.

6. Ethical Reasoning and Tech Awareness

As AI, biotechnology, and automation reshape society, future citizens need a grounding in ethics. What decisions should we delegate to machines? Who is accountable when algorithms fail?

The Role of Educators in the Digital Age

Teachers are no longer just content deliverers. Their roles have evolved to encompass mentorship, emotional support, facilitation, and ethical guidance. In tech-rich environments, the best teachers help students make sense of overwhelming information and maintain human values amid automation.

Professional development for teachers must also keep pace. They need training not just in using edtech, but in understanding its pedagogical impact, biases, and limits. Collaboration between educators, developers, and policymakers is crucial to ensure tech enhances, rather than replaces, good teaching.

Looking Forward

Education 2.0 is not a single system or product. It's a shifting frontier, shaped by technology, economics, politics, and culture. While it offers unprecedented opportunities for personalization, access, and engagement, it also raises tough questions about equity, data, and the human role in a world of machines.

The challenge now is to move beyond hype and gimmicks. Not all digital tools are transformative. Not all automation is progress. We must ask hard questions about purpose: Are we creating systems that serve students, or markets? Are we designing education for empowerment, or efficiency?

If we get it right, Education 2.0 won't just prepare students for the future. It will give them the tools to shape it.

Augmented Reality: Merging the Digital and Physical

Augmented Reality (AR) stands at the forefront of innovation, blurring the boundaries between the virtual and real worlds. It enriches our perception of reality by overlaying digital information onto our physical surroundings. From retail and healthcare to industrial applications, AR promises to revolutionize how we interact with technology and the world around us.

Applications in Retail, Healthcare, and Industry

1. Retail

Augmented Reality has opened new dimensions for the retail industry, transforming how customers shop and experience products. Imagine trying on clothes virtually or visualizing furniture in your living room before making a purchase. Retailers like IKEA have embraced AR to enhance customer engagement and streamline the shopping experience. AR-powered apps allow users to see how items fit in their space, encouraging confident buying decisions.

2. Healthcare

In healthcare, AR holds immense promise for training, surgery, and patient care. Surgeons can use AR to visualize complex anatomy during operations, improving precision and reducing risks. Medical students benefit from immersive simulations that replicate real-world scenarios, accelerating learning without compromising patient safety. AR also aids in rehabilitation by providing interactive exercises and real-time feedback, enhancing recovery outcomes.

3. Industry

Industrial sectors are leveraging AR to optimize workflows, enhance maintenance tasks, and improve safety protocols. Workers equipped with AR-enabled devices can access real-time data overlays, instructions, and remote assistance, minimizing downtime and errors. AR-enhanced training programs allow new employees to learn complex tasks in simulated environments, reducing training costs and improving operational efficiency.

Enhancement of the Physical World with Digital Information

AR enhances our daily interactions by seamlessly integrating digital content into the physical environment. It overlays information, graphics, and interactive elements onto real-world objects, enriching our understanding and engagement.

1. Information Overlay

AR transforms how we access information. By pointing a smartphone or wearable device at an object, users can instantly retrieve relevant data, such as historical facts about landmarks or nutritional information about food products. Museums use AR to provide interactive exhibits, bringing artifacts to life with multimedia content and educational insights.

2. Interactive Experiences

AR fosters immersive and interactive experiences across various domains. From interactive art installations that respond to viewers' movements to location-based games that blend virtual challenges with real-world exploration, AR enriches entertainment and leisure activities. Theme parks and tourism industries incorporate AR to create memorable experiences that engage visitors in new and dynamic ways.

3. Spatial Visualization

Architects, urban planners, and designers use AR to visualize and refine projects in real-world contexts. AR models enable stakeholders to explore proposed buildings, infrastructure developments, and urban designs at scale and in situ. This spatial visualization facilitates collaborative decision-making, enhances design accuracy, and accelerates project timelines.

Risks of Addiction and Distorted Perceptions of Reality

While AR offers transformative benefits, it also poses risks that warrant careful consideration.

1. Digital Addiction

The immersive nature of AR experiences raises concerns about digital addiction. Continuous engagement with augmented environments may lead to excessive screen time and detachment from physical surroundings. Individuals, especially children and adolescents, may struggle to balance virtual interactions with real-world activities, impacting mental well-being and social relationships.

2. Perceptual Distortion

AR blurs the distinction between virtual and real, potentially distorting users' perceptions of reality. Extended exposure to augmented environments may influence cognitive processes and spatial awareness, altering how individuals navigate physical spaces and interpret sensory stimuli. Maintaining a clear distinction between augmented and actual realities is crucial to mitigate perceptual challenges and ensure user safety.

Future Potential in Various Fields

Looking ahead, Augmented Reality holds vast potential to reshape industries and enrich everyday experiences.

1. Education and Training

AR will continue to revolutionize education by offering personalized learning experiences and immersive simulations. Students can explore historical events through interactive AR timelines or conduct virtual science experiments in augmented laboratories. AR-enhanced training programs will empower professionals across diverse sectors, from aviation and engineering to hospitality and customer service.

2. Healthcare Innovation

In healthcare, AR will advance surgical procedures, medical diagnostics, and patient care. Augmented reality glasses equipped with medical imaging overlays will provide surgeons with real-time anatomical guidance during complex surgeries. AR-powered telemedicine platforms will enable remote consultations and virtual examinations, expanding access to specialized healthcare services globally.

3. Remote Collaboration

AR facilitates seamless collaboration among geographically dispersed teams. Professionals can participate in virtual meetings, manipulate shared 3D models, and annotate real-time data overlays, enhancing productivity and communication. Industries ranging from architecture and manufacturing to entertainment and marketing will leverage AR to foster innovation and drive collective creativity.

Conclusion

Augmented Reality represents a transformative force at the intersection of digital innovation and physical reality. By enhancing our perception, interaction and understanding of the world, AR redefines how we work, learn, entertain, and connect. As technology continues to evolve, responsible integration of AR solutions will be essential to harness its full potential while addressing associated risks. Embracing augmented reality promises to usher in a future where digital and physical realms converge harmoniously, enriching human experiences and driving continuous innovation across global industries.

In an increasingly connected world, surveillance technology and data collection have become ubiquitous. From street cameras to social media platforms and mobile devices, the ability to monitor, track, and analyse individuals' activities has expanded at a rapid pace. While these advancements have brought security benefits and convenience, they have also raised significant concerns about privacy, civil liberties, and the potential for abuse. As we navigate this complex landscape, it's crucial to examine the growth of surveillance technology, the delicate balance between security and freedom, public perceptions of privacy intrusion, and the evolving role of legislation in protecting privacy rights.

Growth of Surveillance Technology and Data Collection

The rise of surveillance technology has been driven by rapid advancements in digital infrastructure and the proliferation of data-generating devices. Over the past few decades, we have witnessed an unprecedented increase in the volume and variety of data collected about individuals.

1. CCTV and Public Surveillance

Closed-circuit television (CCTV) cameras, once primarily used in retail and security applications, have become an integral part of urban infrastructure worldwide. According to reports, some cities, especially in countries like China, have reached a level of surveillance where millions of cameras are deployed, constantly monitoring public spaces. These systems are capable of facial recognition, identifying individuals as they move through city streets, shopping malls, or even airports. CCTV surveillance has expanded beyond mere observation to incorporate technologies such as automatic license plate recognition (ALPR) and advanced video analytics, enabling real-time tracking and even predictive policing.

2. Social Media and Data Harvesting

Social media platforms have become some of the most powerful tools for data collection. Every post, like, share, comment, and interaction on platforms such as Facebook, Instagram, and Twitter generates data that companies collect and analyse. This data is used to build detailed profiles of users' preferences, habits, and behaviours. The impact of social media companies' ability to gather and sell data has become a focal point of concern, especially following high-profile scandals like the Cambridge Analytica incident. The explosion of data collection extends beyond social media, with apps on smartphones, smart home devices, and even wearables continually collecting information about users' locations, activities, health metrics, and even conversations.

3. Biometric Data and Facial Recognition

Biometric technology has made significant strides, particularly in the realm of facial recognition. Governments, law enforcement agencies, and private corporations have begun implementing facial recognition software as part of security measures in airports, government buildings, public transportation systems, and even shopping centres. This technology is designed to identify individuals in real-time by analyzing unique facial features. While touted as an efficient means of enhancing security and preventing crime, facial recognition has sparked debates over its accuracy, reliability, and potential for misuse.

In addition to facial recognition, other forms of biometric surveillance, including fingerprinting, iris scans, and voice recognition, have also become more widespread. These technologies are often used to enhance security in both physical and digital spaces. However, the ability to track individuals through biometric identifiers has raised concerns about the potential for widespread surveillance and data breaches.

Balancing Security with Civil Liberties

One of the central issues in the debate over surveillance technology is finding a balance between national security or public safety and the protection of individual freedoms. Security measures, such as surveillance cameras and data collection, are often justified on the grounds of crime prevention, terrorism detection, and public safety. Governments argue that surveillance is necessary to ensure the security of citizens and to maintain law and order.

1. Security as a Justification

After events like the September 11th terrorist attacks, many governments worldwide adopted more aggressive surveillance strategies, citing national security concerns. Measures such as mass data collection, expanded surveillance of communication networks, and the use of intelligence agencies to monitor individuals have become more common. Proponents argue that these measures help prevent terrorism, organized crime, and other threats. The growth of smart cities and the expansion of connected infrastructure, such as IoT devices, also provide more opportunities for real-time monitoring and emergency responses to crises.

2. The Risk of Overreach

However, the challenge arises when the mechanisms designed to protect citizens begin to infringe on fundamental civil liberties, such as the right to privacy, freedom of expression, and due process. Governments and organizations often overreach in their surveillance efforts, collecting more data than necessary and using invasive technologies that can target innocent individuals without cause. The use of mass data collection tools like phone tracking, email monitoring, and online activity tracking can result in disproportionate surveillance of vulnerable populations, leading to unjust profiling and discrimination.

The line between necessary security measures and the erosion of personal freedoms becomes especially thin when governments use surveillance technology for political purposes, such as monitoring dissent or curbing opposition. The impact of surveillance is even more pronounced when it is used to suppress free speech, assemble peacefully, or engage in activism. As governments amass large volumes of personal data, the question arises: how much surveillance is acceptable in a free society?

Public Perception and Response to Privacy Intrusion

The increasing ubiquity of surveillance has generated a significant public debate over privacy and the right to control one's personal information. While many people are willing to trade some degree of privacy for increased security or convenience, there are growing concerns about the loss of control over personal data.

1. Willingness to Trade Privacy for Security

Surveys and studies have shown that public opinion on surveillance varies depending on the context. Many people are willing to accept surveillance measures if they believe they will enhance security, prevent crime, or protect against terrorism. For example, the public's willingness to accept the use of facial recognition technology in airports or high-security areas may be high due to the perceived benefits in preventing terrorist attacks or criminal activity.

However, the growing awareness of data collection by corporations has led to increasing skepticism about the motives behind surveillance. With frequent revelations about how companies sell or misuse data, many individuals are becoming more cautious about what they share and with whom. The recent rise of privacy-focused technologies, such as encrypted communication apps and secure search engines, reflects this shift in public sentiment.

2. Public Backlash and Privacy Movements

In response to growing concerns about privacy invasion, advocacy groups, privacy experts, and tech companies have been pushing for greater transparency and accountability in surveillance practices. Movements such as "Stop the Surveillance State" and campaigns for stronger data protection laws highlight the need to safeguard privacy rights in an increasingly interconnected world.

Public outcry has led to legislative changes in some regions, and major companies, such as Google and Apple, have introduced privacy-focused features, including transparent data usage policies and stronger encryption methods. However, these efforts often fall short of addressing the broader issues of mass surveillance and government overreach.

The Role of Legislation in Protecting Privacy Rights

As surveillance technologies continue to advance, governments and international bodies must enact legislation to protect individuals' privacy rights. Striking a balance between security and civil liberties requires the establishment of clear guidelines regarding data collection, storage, and usage, as well as oversight of surveillance activities.

1. Global Privacy Regulations

Around the world, privacy regulations are being introduced to limit the scope of data collection and enhance individuals' control over their personal information. The European Union's General Data Protection Regulation (GDPR) is one of the most comprehensive privacy laws, requiring companies to be transparent about how they collect, store, and use personal data. The GDPR has set a global standard for privacy protection, forcing businesses to reconsider how they handle consumer information.

The California Consumer Privacy Act (CCPA) is another significant piece of legislation in the United States that aims to give individuals more control over their personal data. Similar laws are being considered or implemented in other regions as well, though there remains a significant disparity between different countries' approaches to data privacy.

2. Surveillance and Oversight

In addition to privacy regulations, laws governing the use of surveillance technology, particularly by government agencies, are essential. There must be clear rules about when and how surveillance can be conducted, who is authorized to monitor individuals, and how long data can be retained. Independent oversight bodies and transparency measures, such as public audits, can help ensure that surveillance is used appropriately and not for political or discriminatory purposes.

As surveillance technology becomes more advanced, it will be essential for lawmakers to keep pace with developments in technology. This may include addressing emerging concerns related to AI-powered surveillance, biometric data, and cross-border data flows. The role of international cooperation in data protection will also become increasingly important, especially in an era where personal information can easily transcend national borders.

Conclusion

The growth of surveillance technology and data collection presents both opportunities and challenges. While these tools have the potential to enhance security, streamline services, and improve efficiency, they also raise profound questions about privacy, individual freedoms, and the role of government oversight. Striking the right balance between security and civil liberties will require ongoing dialogue between governments, tech companies, advocacy groups, and the public. In an age where privacy is increasingly becoming a commodity, safeguarding individual rights and freedoms will be one of the most important tasks of the digital age. The future of privacy and surveillance will depend on the strength of the protections we put in place today and the awareness we bring to these issues as technology continues to evolve.

Blockchain technology has gained significant attention in recent years, often associated with cryptocurrencies like Bitcoin and Ethereum. However, its potential extends far beyond digital currencies, offering transformative possibilities in various sectors. Blockchain's decentralized, transparent, and immutable nature promises to redefine the way trust is established in both digital and physical worlds. This chapter explores the core principles of blockchain technology, its applications beyond cryptocurrencies, the quest for decentralization of power, and the challenges it faces in terms of scalability and widespread adoption.

Introduction and Definition of Blockchain Technology

At its core, blockchain is a distributed ledger technology (DLT) that enables secure, transparent, and tamper-resistant record-keeping without the need for a central authority. Each block in the blockchain contains a list of transactions that are cryptographically linked to the previous block, forming a chain. This structure ensures that once data is recorded, it cannot be altered without changing every subsequent block, making the blockchain immutable and secure.

Unlike traditional centralized systems, where a single entity, such as a bank or government, oversees the validation of transactions, blockchain operates in a decentralized manner. Multiple participants, or "nodes," validate transactions and maintain copies of the ledger, ensuring transparency and eliminating the risk of a single point of failure. This decentralization removes the need for intermediaries, reducing costs and increasing trust among parties who may not know each other.

Blockchain's security is maintained through cryptographic algorithms, which ensure that only authorized parties can access or modify the data. The most well-known of these algorithms is the consensus mechanism, which ensures that all participants in the network agree on the state of the blockchain. Proof of Work (PoW) and Proof of Stake (PoS) are two of the most widely used consensus mechanisms, each with its own strengths and weaknesses.

Blockchain technology emerged with the advent of Bitcoin in 2009, created by an anonymous individual or group of individuals using the pseudonym Satoshi Nakamoto. Bitcoin used blockchain to solve the problem of double-spending in digital currency, where a person could potentially spend the same money more than once in a digital environment. The success of Bitcoin and the underlying blockchain technology sparked interest in the potential applications of blockchain beyond cryptocurrencies.

Applications Beyond Cryptocurrencies

While cryptocurrencies remain the most well-known application of blockchain, the technology's potential is far broader. Many industries are exploring how blockchain can be used to streamline processes, improve transparency, and increase efficiency. Some of the most promising applications of blockchain technology are found in supply chain management, voting systems, healthcare, and digital identity management.

1. Supply Chain Management

One of the most exciting applications of blockchain is in supply chain management. Traditional supply chains are often complex and involve multiple intermediaries, leading to inefficiencies, fraud, and lack of transparency. Blockchain can provide a solution by creating a transparent and immutable record of every transaction that takes place along the supply chain.

For example, blockchain can be used to track the journey of a product from its origin to the end consumer. By recording each step of the product's journey—whether it's raw materials, manufacturing, shipping, or retail—blockchain enables all parties in the supply chain to have real-time access to accurate data. This transparency can help reduce fraud, prevent counterfeit goods, and ensure that products meet regulatory standards.

In addition to improving transparency, blockchain can also enhance efficiency by automating processes through smart contracts. These self-executing contracts automatically execute terms and conditions when predefined criteria are met, reducing the need for intermediaries and manual verification.

2. Voting Systems

Another critical application of blockchain is in the realm of voting. Traditional voting systems, whether for elections or corporate governance, are often vulnerable to fraud, tampering, and human error. Blockchain's transparency and immutability can help ensure the integrity of voting systems by providing a secure, auditable, and tamper-proof record of votes.

In a blockchain-based voting system, each vote could be recorded as a transaction on the blockchain, with each voter's identity verified through digital signatures or biometric authentication. Once a vote is cast, it cannot be changed or deleted, ensuring that the final tally is accurate and transparent. The decentralized nature of blockchain also makes it difficult for any single entity to manipulate or alter the results.

Blockchain-based voting has the potential to reduce the costs and logistical challenges associated with traditional voting methods, such as paper ballots and physical polling stations. Additionally, it could make voting more accessible by allowing people to vote remotely, increasing voter participation and engagement.

3. Healthcare

In the healthcare sector, blockchain can be used to secure and manage patient data. Medical records are often stored in centralized databases that are vulnerable to breaches, hacking, and unauthorized access. Blockchain offers a way to store medical data securely, ensuring that only authorized parties can access sensitive information.

A blockchain-based system could allow patients to control access to their medical records, sharing them with doctors, hospitals, and other healthcare providers as needed. Each time a record is accessed or updated, a transaction could be recorded on the blockchain, providing a complete and transparent audit trail. This level of transparency can help improve trust between patients and healthcare providers while also reducing administrative costs and improving the accuracy of medical records.

Blockchain could also be used to track the provenance of pharmaceuticals, ensuring that drugs are not counterfeit and are safely distributed to consumers. This application could help combat the global issue of counterfeit drugs, which are a significant threat to public health.

4. Digital Identity Management

As more services and transactions move online, the need for secure and efficient digital identity management has become increasingly important. Traditional identity systems often rely on centralized databases that are vulnerable to hacking and data breaches. Blockchain technology offers a decentralized solution to identity management that is more secure, transparent, and user-controlled.

Blockchain-based identity systems can give individuals greater control over their personal information, allowing them to share only the data they choose with trusted parties. For example, a person could use a blockchain-based identity system to prove their age, citizenship, or academic credentials without revealing sensitive information like their full name or address. This level of privacy and security is difficult to achieve with traditional identity systems.

The Quest for Decentralization of Power

One of the central promises of blockchain technology is its ability to decentralize power. Traditional systems of governance, finance, and commerce rely on central authorities, such as banks, governments, and corporations, to mediate transactions and ensure trust. Blockchain challenges this model by allowing individuals and organizations to interact directly with each other, without the need for intermediaries.

Decentralization has the potential to democratize many aspects of society, including finance, healthcare, and governance. By removing intermediaries, blockchain can reduce the costs and inefficiencies associated with centralized systems, as well as increase transparency and accountability. This is particularly important in contexts where trust in central authorities is low, such as in regions with weak institutions or corrupt governments.

However, decentralization also poses challenges. While blockchain removes the need for intermediaries, it also raises questions about governance. Who decides the rules of the blockchain network? How are decisions made in decentralized systems? In the case of blockchain-based cryptocurrencies, decisions are often made by a community of users, but this can lead to disputes and forks in the network. These governance challenges need to be addressed for blockchain to achieve its full potential as a tool for decentralizing power.

Challenges in Scalability and Adoption

While blockchain offers a wide range of potential applications, there are several challenges that must be addressed before the technology can be widely adopted.

1. Scalability

One of the primary challenges facing blockchain technology is scalability. Traditional blockchain networks, particularly those that use Proof of Work (PoW) as a consensus mechanism, can only process a limited number of transactions per second. Bitcoin, for example, can handle around seven transactions per second, while traditional payment networks like Visa can handle thousands.

As blockchain technology grows in popularity and is applied to more use cases, scalability becomes an increasingly important issue. Solutions like the Lightning Network for Bitcoin and Ethereum's transition to Proof of Stake (PoS) are designed to address these scalability challenges by enabling faster transactions and reducing the energy consumption associated with mining. However, these solutions are still in development and have yet to be widely implemented.

2. Adoption and Integration

Another significant barrier to the widespread adoption of blockchain is the integration of the technology into existing systems and infrastructure. Many organizations are hesitant to adopt blockchain due to its complexity and the need to re-engineer their processes. Furthermore, there are concerns about the regulatory environment surrounding blockchain, as many countries are still grappling with how to classify and regulate the technology.

Additionally, blockchain requires a shift in mindset. Traditional systems rely on centralized authorities to enforce trust and resolve disputes. Blockchain, on the other hand, relies on decentralized consensus and cryptographic trust. This shift can be difficult for organizations and individuals to embrace, particularly when it comes to replacing established practices and institutions.

Conclusion

Blockchain technology represents a fundamental shift in how we think about trust, transparency, and decentralization. While cryptocurrencies remain the most well-known application, blockchain's potential extends far beyond digital currencies. From supply chain management to voting systems, healthcare, and digital identity management, blockchain has the power to transform many sectors by increasing efficiency, transparency, and security.

However, the journey towards widespread adoption is not without challenges. Issues such as scalability, governance, and integration into existing systems must be addressed before blockchain can fully realize its potential. As the technology continues to evolve, it will likely play a central role in redefining the way we establish trust in the digital age. The blockchain revolution is just beginning, and its impact on society will be felt for years to come.

In the digital age, where an increasing portion of our personal, financial, and professional lives is conducted online, cybersecurity has become one of the most critical concerns. The rise of sophisticated cyberattacks, data breaches, and identity theft has created a climate of constant vigilance. As individuals and organizations store vast amounts of sensitive information online, protecting that data has become a paramount concern for governments, businesses, and individuals alike.

This chapter explores the growing threats in cyberspace, the evolution of cybersecurity measures, the importance of public awareness and education, and the emerging technologies that promise to enhance cybersecurity in the future.

Rising Threats in Cyberspace

The threat landscape in cyberspace is constantly evolving, with attackers becoming more sophisticated and persistent. Cybercrime is now a multibillion-dollar industry, with various malicious actors ranging from lone hackers to organized crime syndicates and even state-sponsored groups. The internet, which was once seen as an open and secure space for communication, commerce, and information-sharing, is now a battleground where data sovereignty is under constant attack.

1. Hacking

Hacking, the unauthorized access to computer systems, remains one of the most significant threats to cybersecurity. Hackers use various techniques, such as exploiting vulnerabilities in software, phishing, or brute-force attacks, to infiltrate systems and steal sensitive data. These attacks can target both individuals and organizations, often with devastating consequences. For instance, hackers may steal credit card information, intellectual property, or personal health records, which can lead to identity theft, financial loss, or reputational damage.

One of the most notable types of hacking is **ransomware**, a form of malicious software (malware) that locks users out of their systems or encrypts their data, demanding a ransom for its release. Ransomware attacks have surged in recent years, targeting high-profile entities such as hospitals, schools, and government agencies. The increasing sophistication of ransomware attacks, coupled with the growing number of victims, has made them a significant concern in the cybersecurity space.

2. Identity Theft

Identity theft occurs when an attacker gains unauthorized access to an individual's personal information, such as their Social Security number, bank account details, or login credentials. Once the hacker has this information, they can commit fraud by opening credit accounts, draining bank accounts, or impersonating the victim to gain access to additional resources.

With the advent of digital technologies, identity theft has become more prevalent and harder to detect. The rise of data breaches in which large amounts of personal information are exposed has led to a sharp increase in the number of identity theft cases. Cybercriminals can buy and sell stolen data on the dark web, enabling them to use it for malicious purposes.

3. Phishing and Social Engineering

Phishing is a form of cyberattack where attackers attempt to trick individuals into revealing sensitive information, such as usernames, passwords, or financial details. This is typically done by posing as a trusted entity, such as a bank, government agency, or popular online service, and sending fraudulent emails, messages, or phone calls that appear legitimate.

Social engineering is closely related to phishing but involves manipulating individuals into divulging confidential information. This can take the form of pretexting (where an attacker pretends to be someone else), baiting (offering something attractive to get the victim to engage), or tailgating (gaining physical access to a restricted area by following authorized personnel). Social engineering exploits human psychology, making it one of the most dangerous forms of cyberattack.

4. State-Sponsored Cyberattacks

In addition to individual hackers and criminal organizations, nation-states have become significant players in the cyber threat landscape. State-sponsored cyberattacks are often politically motivated and target critical infrastructure, government agencies, private companies, and even individuals. These attacks can range from cyber-espionage, where sensitive government or corporate data is stolen, to cyberwarfare, which aims to disrupt or destroy an adversary's infrastructure.

One example of state-sponsored cyberattacks is the **NotPetya** attack in 2017, which targeted Ukrainian organizations but also spread globally, causing widespread damage. This attack was widely attributed to Russian-backed hackers and was seen as an example of the increasing use of cyberattacks as a tool of geopolitical conflict.

Evolution of Security Measures and Responses

As the threats in cyberspace have evolved, so too have the measures to protect against them. Early cybersecurity focused primarily on securing individual computers and networks through firewalls, antivirus software, and encryption. However, as the scope of cyber threats has expanded, the approach to cybersecurity has had to evolve.

1. Traditional Security Measures

Traditional security measures, such as firewalls and antivirus programs, have played a significant role in protecting computers and networks from attacks. Firewalls act as a barrier between a trusted internal network and untrusted external networks, filtering incoming and outgoing traffic based on predefined rules. Antivirus software scans for and removes malicious programs that could compromise the security of a system.

While these measures are still important, they are no longer sufficient on their own, particularly as cyberattacks become more sophisticated. Firewalls and antivirus programs are reactive—they can only detect and respond to threats once they have been identified. Hackers are constantly adapting and finding ways to bypass traditional security defences.

2. Multi-Factor Authentication (MFA)

One of the most effective ways to secure digital identities is through **multi-factor authentication (MFA)**. MFA requires users to provide multiple forms of identification before gaining access to a system or service. Typically, this involves something the user knows (a password), something the user has (a smartphone or hardware token), and something the user is (biometric data such as a fingerprint or face scan).

By requiring multiple forms of authentication, MFA significantly reduces the risk of unauthorized access, even if an attacker manages to steal a password. As a result, MFA has become a standard security feature for many online services, particularly those that handle sensitive information, such as banking or healthcare services.

3. Artificial Intelligence and Machine Learning in Cybersecurity

As cyber threats have become more complex and dynamic, cybersecurity professionals have turned to artificial intelligence (AI) and machine learning (ML) to help detect and respond to attacks. AI-powered systems can analyze vast amounts of data in real-time, identifying patterns and anomalies that may indicate a cyberattack.

For example, AI algorithms can monitor network traffic and detect unusual activity, such as large data transfers or unauthorized access attempts. Machine learning models can also learn from past attacks, improving their ability to predict and prevent future threats. These technologies have the potential to revolutionize cybersecurity by providing proactive, real-time protection against emerging threats.

4. Blockchain for Cybersecurity

Blockchain technology, with its decentralized and tamper-resistant nature, has found applications in cybersecurity. Blockchain can enhance data integrity by ensuring that records are immutable and traceable. It can also be used to create more secure authentication systems, where users' credentials are stored in a decentralized manner, reducing the risk of centralized databases being hacked.

In addition, blockchain-based systems can be used to secure transactions in online environments, such as financial transactions or digital contracts, by providing a transparent and tamper-proof record of all interactions.

The Importance of Public Awareness and Education

As cyber threats become more prevalent, public awareness and education are critical components of a comprehensive cybersecurity strategy. Many cyberattacks are successful because individuals unknowingly engage in risky online behaviour, such as clicking on phishing links, using weak passwords, or neglecting to update software regularly.

Educating the public about the importance of cybersecurity and how to protect themselves is essential to reducing the risk of cyberattacks. This education should include teaching individuals about basic cybersecurity practices, such as:

- Using strong, unique passwords for each online account
- Enabling multi-factor authentication where possible
- Being cautious when clicking on links or downloading attachments from unknown sources
- Regularly updating software and security patches
- Recognizing common phishing tactics and social engineering schemes

Governments, educational institutions, and private organizations all play a role in promoting cybersecurity awareness. By providing resources, training, and support, we can equip individuals with the knowledge and skills needed to protect themselves in an increasingly connected world.

Future Technologies for Enhanced Cybersecurity

The future of cybersecurity will likely see continued advancements in both technology and strategy, driven by the evolving threat landscape. Several emerging technologies have the potential to revolutionize how we protect data and digital infrastructure.

1. Quantum Cryptography

Quantum computing has the potential to break many of the encryption methods that currently secure data. However, it also holds promise for creating new forms of encryption that are virtually impossible to crack. **Quantum cryptography** uses the principles of quantum mechanics to create encryption keys that are theoretically unbreakable. These keys are based on the behaviour of quantum particles, which are highly sensitive to any interference, making it nearly impossible for an attacker to intercept or alter the data without detection.

As quantum computing technology advances, quantum cryptography could become a vital tool in securing sensitive data and communications.

2. Zero Trust Architecture

Zero Trust is an evolving cybersecurity framework that assumes that no one, whether inside or outside the network, can be trusted by default. Instead of assuming that users or devices within an organization's network are trustworthy, Zero Trust requires continuous verification of identity, device health, and behaviour before granting access to sensitive resources.

Zero Trust architecture is designed to minimize the risk of data breaches by ensuring that every access request is rigorously authenticated and authorized, regardless of where it originates. This approach is gaining traction as more organizations shift to cloud-based systems and remote work environments.

Conclusion

As the digital world continues to evolve, cybersecurity will remain a critical area of focus. With the rise of hacking, identity theft, ransomware, and state-sponsored cyberattacks, the need for robust security measures has never been greater. From traditional defences like firewalls and antivirus software to advanced technologies like AI, blockchain, and quantum cryptography, the cybersecurity landscape is constantly shifting to meet new challenges.

However, technology alone is not enough. Public awareness and education about cybersecurity best practices are essential in empowering individuals to protect themselves online. As we move forward, a collaborative approach—combining technological innovation, education, and responsible governance—will be necessary to ensure data sovereignty and safeguard the integrity of our digital lives. The battle for data sovereignty is ongoing, and it will require continuous adaptation to stay one step ahead of those who seek to exploit the vulnerabilities of cyberspace.

The 21st century is witnessing a seismic shift in how humans move from place to place. Transportation, a backbone of modern civilization, is undergoing a radical transformation driven by advances in automation, electrification, and intelligent systems. At the centre of this change are autonomous vehicles (AVs), but they are only one part of a broader reimagining of transit that includes hyperloops, aerial mobility, and smart infrastructure. As the lines between digital and physical continue to blur, transportation is evolving into a dynamic, interconnected ecosystem.

This chapter delves into the evolution of self-driving vehicles, explores cutting-edge transit innovations, evaluates the risks associated with automating our daily commute, and reflects on how cities and societies are reshaping themselves around new mobility paradigms.

Development of Self-Driving Cars and Their Impact

Self-driving cars, also known as autonomous vehicles (AVs), are no longer confined to science fiction. Leveraging a fusion of AI, machine learning, LIDAR, radar, and GPS, these vehicles are designed to navigate roads with little to no human intervention. Companies like Waymo, Tesla, Cruise, and Baidu have invested billions into developing fully autonomous systems that promise to change the way we drive, commute, and interact with vehicles.

Autonomous driving technology is typically classified into five levels, from Level 0 (no automation) to Level 5 (full automation). Most commercial vehicles today fall between Levels 2 and 3, offering partial automation such as adaptive cruise control, lane-keeping, and self-parking features. Level 4 and 5 vehicles, capable of navigating without any driver input, are still in testing phases and limited deployments.

The potential benefits are significant. AVs could reduce traffic accidents—over 90% of which are caused by human error. They offer mobility to those unable to drive, such as the elderly and disabled, and could lower emissions through optimized driving patterns and coordinated traffic flow.

However, the transition to autonomy isn't seamless. Safety concerns linger after high-profile accidents involving self-driving cars. Ethical dilemmas—such as decision-making in unavoidable crash scenarios—highlight the complexity of programming morality into machines. Furthermore, job displacement in sectors like trucking and taxi services poses socio-economic challenges.

Despite these hurdles, the trajectory toward autonomy seems inevitable, particularly as data and compute power grow more capable. The challenge lies in ensuring that the transition is safe, equitable, and beneficial across all layers of society.

Transit Innovations: Hyperloops, Drones, and Flying Taxis

Beyond autonomous vehicles, a wave of transportation innovations is pushing boundaries previously thought unreachable. One such concept is the **hyperloop**—a high-speed transport system proposed by Elon Musk in 2013. Utilizing vacuum tubes and magnetic levitation, hyperloops aim to move passenger pods at speeds exceeding 700 mph. Prototypes and feasibility studies are underway in the U.S., UAE, and Europe, though commercial deployment remains years away.

Another rapidly advancing field is **aerial mobility**, which includes autonomous drones and flying taxis. Companies like Joby Aviation, Volocopter, and EHang are developing vertical take-off and landing (VTOL) vehicles intended for short urban flights. These electric air taxis could drastically reduce commute times, particularly in congested cities, and open up new possibilities for emergency response, cargo transport, and tourism.

Delivery drones are also finding their place in modern logistics. Amazon, UPS, and various startups are testing drone delivery systems that can transport packages over short distances quickly and with minimal human involvement. In remote or hard-to-reach areas, drones can be a lifeline for delivering medical supplies, food, or emergency aid.

Smart infrastructure is key to supporting these innovations. Sensors, real-time data analytics, and AI-driven traffic systems can optimize routes, prevent congestion, and enable vehicle-to-infrastructure communication. This intelligent connectivity turns roads and skies into integrated, adaptive environments where safety and efficiency are prioritized.

Risks of Reliance on Automation in Commuting

While automation offers clear benefits, it also introduces a set of new risks that cannot be ignored. One of the primary concerns is **system vulnerability**. A reliance on software and digital networks exposes transportation systems to cyberattacks, malfunctions, and data breaches. A single exploit could disrupt entire traffic networks or hijack vehicles.

Another challenge is **technological dependence**. As more commuters place trust in autonomous systems, there's a risk of skills erosion. Drivers who become too reliant on automation may lose the ability to respond appropriately in emergency scenarios. Over-trust in machines could foster complacency.

Decision-making transparency is also an issue. AVs rely on complex algorithms that are often opaque to users and regulators. Understanding how and why an autonomous system makes a certain decision—especially during an accident—can be difficult, leading to questions about accountability and liability.

There are also concerns about **data privacy**. As autonomous and smart vehicles collect vast amounts of data on user behaviour, location, and preferences, questions arise about who owns this data and how it's used. Without strong regulatory frameworks, personal data could be exploited for commercial or even malicious purposes.

Equity and access present further issues. High-tech transit solutions often emerge first in affluent urban areas, potentially leaving rural or underserved communities behind. If automation benefits only the wealthy or tech-savvy, it risks exacerbating existing inequalities.

The Changing Landscape of Urban Transportation

Cities are not static; they evolve alongside technology and societal needs. As autonomous vehicles and new transport modes become more prevalent, urban landscapes are adapting accordingly. One visible trend is the **reduction of car ownership** in favour of shared, on-demand services. Ride-hailing platforms like Uber and Lyft have already begun this shift, and autonomous fleets may accelerate it.

This transition impacts **urban planning**. Cities may need fewer parking lots and gas stations, freeing up valuable real estate for parks, housing, or community spaces. Roads may be redesigned for smoother autonomous traffic flow, while infrastructure such as dedicated AV lanes, drone landing pads, and hyperloop stations begin to take shape.

Public transport is also undergoing a transformation. Smart buses, app-based ticketing, and AI-driven scheduling are improving efficiency and convenience. Micro-mobility options, such as e-scooters and bike-sharing, are being integrated into broader transit networks, offering flexible last-mile solutions.

Environmental considerations play a significant role. Electric autonomous vehicles could reduce emissions, but this depends heavily on the source of electricity and lifecycle emissions of manufacturing and disposing of vehicles. Sustainable transportation isn't just about innovation; it's about ensuring those innovations are truly green.

Policy and governance are crucial in shaping this future. Cities must create frameworks that encourage innovation while protecting public interests. This includes updating traffic laws, investing in infrastructure, regulating data use, and ensuring that new technologies serve diverse populations.

Ultimately, the goal is not merely faster or fancier transit but **smarter mobility—** a system that is efficient, inclusive, sustainable, and resilient.

Conclusion

The transportation sector is standing at a crossroads, with emerging technologies poised to redefine how we move through the world. Autonomous vehicles are leading the charge, but the broader narrative includes flying taxis, high-speed hyperloops, delivery drones, and intelligent infrastructure. These innovations promise convenience, efficiency, and safety, but they also come with profound risks and societal implications.

The path forward requires a balance between embracing the future and safeguarding against its potential downsides. By investing in robust infrastructure, ensuring equitable access, promoting public awareness, and enacting thoughtful policies, society can navigate this transformation in a way that benefits all.

The gig economy has become one of the defining shifts in the global labour landscape over the past two decades. Characterized by short-term contracts, freelance work, and on-demand jobs facilitated by digital platforms, this model has redefined what it means to work in the 21st century. With platforms like Uber, Deliveroo, Fiverr, and TaskRabbit leading the charge, the gig economy offers workers a new level of flexibility and independence—yet raises critical questions about job security, workers' rights, and the future of employment itself.

Definition and Rise of the Gig Economy

The term "gig economy" originates from the music industry, where performers would go from one short-term engagement—or "gig"—to another. Today, the concept has expanded far beyond creative professions. The gig economy encompasses a broad range of work arrangements where individuals earn income through temporary, flexible jobs, often mediated through digital platforms.

This economic model has surged thanks to several converging trends:

- **Digital Connectivity:** The proliferation of smartphones and mobile apps has made it easier than ever for people to find and offer services.

- **Economic Pressures:** The 2008 global financial crisis pushed many toward freelance or gig work out of necessity. A similar pattern was observed during the COVID-19 pandemic.

- **Cultural Shifts:** Many younger workers prioritize autonomy and flexibility over traditional 9-to-5 structures.

- **Platform Innovation:** Companies like Airbnb and Uber built digital marketplaces that seamlessly connect demand and supply in real time.

Today, millions of workers around the world participate in the gig economy, either as their primary source of income or to supplement traditional employment.

Flexibility vs. Job Security Implications

One of the biggest selling points of the gig economy is flexibility. Workers can often set their own schedules, choose how much or little they work, and operate from almost anywhere. For students, parents, or people with other commitments, this autonomy is invaluable. It allows a level of personal agency that rigid corporate structures rarely provide.

However, this freedom comes at a cost.

Lack of Benefits

Gig workers typically do not receive benefits that are standard in traditional employment, such as health insurance, paid leave, or retirement plans. This makes them more vulnerable, especially during economic downturns or personal health crises.

Income Instability

Earnings in the gig economy can be highly unpredictable. Workers may face dry spells with little to no work, fierce competition that drives down wages, or sudden platform algorithm changes that affect their visibility and income.

Power Imbalance

Although gig work may seem like self-employment, many workers are still heavily reliant on the platforms that distribute gigs. These companies often set terms unilaterally, enforce performance metrics, and take significant commissions—all without granting workers the status of formal employees.

The result is a precarious work environment where flexibility masks deeper instability.

The Impact on Traditional Employment Structures

The rise of gig work has not occurred in a vacuum. It has fundamentally altered the employment landscape, with ripple effects across sectors.

Erosion of Long-Term Employment

As gig platforms grow, they often undercut traditional businesses that rely on salaried workers. Taxi companies, for instance, have lost market share to rideshare apps that rely on independent contractors. Similarly, freelance marketplaces are replacing full-time creative departments in some firms.

Reimagining the Workplace

Companies are increasingly outsourcing tasks to gig workers rather than hiring new employees. This allows them to reduce overhead costs and scale operations more easily. While this may improve efficiency, it also diminishes the traditional employer-employee relationship, weakening loyalty and long-term investment in workers.

Influence on Labor Markets

The gig model encourages a shift toward project-based thinking. Job descriptions are being restructured around deliverables rather than roles, and performance is often evaluated per task. This reorientation could lead to a more dynamic and adaptable workforce, but also one where individuals are constantly hustling for the next job.

Future of Labour and Worker Rights

The gig economy raises urgent questions about how society defines work and what protections workers should be entitled to in an increasingly digital labor market.

Legal Classification Battles

A major debate centers on whether gig workers should be classified as employees or independent contractors. The distinction is crucial, as it determines eligibility for benefits, protections, and labor rights.

Some jurisdictions have started to address this. In California, Assembly Bill 5 (AB5) aimed to reclassify many gig workers as employees. While the legislation faced legal challenges and was later modified by Proposition 22 (backed by gig economy firms), it marked a pivotal moment in the conversation around gig work.

Platform Accountability

As digital platforms become central labour intermediaries, calls for greater accountability grow louder. Should Uber be responsible for the well-being of its drivers? Should Fiverr ensure fair pay for freelancers? Without regulation, these platforms operate in a grey area, profiting from labour without assuming employer responsibilities.

Universal Basic Income and New Safety Nets

One proposed solution to gig economy precarity is the implementation of Universal Basic Income (UBI)—a guaranteed financial floor for all citizens. Others advocate for portable benefits systems that would follow workers across gigs and platforms. These ideas aim to decouple social protections from traditional employment.

Empowering Workers Through Technology

New digital tools are emerging to support gig workers. Apps that track income, manage taxes, or pool benefits are giving workers more control. Worker cooperatives and unions are also forming to negotiate better terms with platforms.

Still, these efforts are fragmented and often lack the scale to counterbalance powerful tech firms.

A Dual-Edged Sword

The gig economy embodies both promise and peril. On one hand, it offers a flexible and potentially empowering model for work in the digital age. On the other, it threatens to erode the hard-won protections that defined 20th-century labour rights.

Moving forward, the challenge is not to resist the gig economy but to reshape it. That means designing policies, technologies, and cultural norms that ensure fairness, dignity, and stability—even in nontraditional work arrangements.

Governments, platforms, and society at large must grapple with the paradox at the heart of gig work: the same systems that enable freedom can also entrench inequality. How we resolve this tension will shape the nature of work—and the lives of workers—for generations to come.

As the global population continues to grow—expected to exceed 9 billion by 2050—ensuring a sustainable, nutritious, and equitable food supply is one of the century's most urgent challenges. Traditional agricultural methods, while effective in the past, are no longer sufficient to meet this demand without causing significant environmental degradation. Food technology is rapidly emerging as a transformative force in rethinking how we produce, distribute, and consume food.

From lab-grown meat and vertical farming to AI-driven logistics and smart packaging, the food industry is undergoing a technological revolution. But with these advances come pressing questions: Can technology solve global hunger? What are the ethical implications of artificial food? And how do we ensure these innovations benefit everyone, not just the wealthy few?

Advances in Agriculture and Food Production

Technological innovation in agriculture has been instrumental in increasing food production while attempting to reduce environmental impact.

Vertical Farming

Vertical farming is the practice of growing crops in vertically stacked layers, often within controlled indoor environments. Utilizing LED lighting, hydroponics, and climate control systems, vertical farms allow for year-round production without the need for pesticides or vast land use. Because they can be located in urban centres, vertical farms also reduce transportation emissions and provide fresh produce directly to local populations.

Companies like AeroFarms, Plenty, and Bowery Farming are leading the charge, demonstrating how urban agriculture can reduce dependency on rural farmland and unpredictable climate conditions. Moreover, these systems use up to 95% less water than traditional farming, a significant benefit in an era of increasing water scarcity.

Lab-Grown Meat

Also known as cultured or cell-based meat, lab-grown meat is created by cultivating animal cells in bioreactors, bypassing the need to raise and slaughter animals. This approach significantly reduces land and water usage and emits far fewer greenhouse gases than conventional livestock farming.

Startups such as Mosa Meat, Upside Foods, and Eat Just are developing meat products that mimic the taste and texture of real meat while being more ethical and sustainable. While still expensive and in the early stages of commercial availability, lab-grown meat holds promise as a scalable solution to the environmental and ethical issues of animal agriculture.

Genetic Engineering and CRISPR

Genetic editing tools like CRISPR are being used to enhance crop resilience, nutritional value, and shelf life. Scientists can now create plants that are drought-tolerant, disease-resistant, or rich in specific vitamins, helping to combat malnutrition and food insecurity.

Golden Rice, for example, is genetically engineered to produce vitamin A and is aimed at reducing childhood blindness and mortality in developing countries. However, these innovations are not without controversy, particularly around public acceptance and regulatory hurdles.

Innovations in Supply Chain and Food Distribution

Producing food is only one part of the equation. Equally important is the ability to distribute it efficiently and safely.

Blockchain for Traceability

Blockchain technology is increasingly being used to create transparent, tamper-proof supply chains. With blockchain, every step of a food item's journey—from farm to fork—can be recorded and verified. This enhances food safety, reduces fraud, and increases consumer trust.

Companies like IBM Food Trust are partnering with major retailers such as Walmart and Carrefour to implement blockchain-based tracking systems. Consumers can scan a QR code on a product to see where it was grown, how it was transported, and when it was harvested.

AI and Predictive Analytics

Artificial intelligence is revolutionizing inventory management and demand forecasting. Retailers and suppliers use AI to predict buying patterns, optimize stock levels, and reduce spoilage. This minimizes food waste and ensures that perishable items are delivered in optimal condition.

Robotics and automation are also playing an increasing role in logistics, from autonomous delivery vehicles to AI-controlled warehouse systems. These innovations improve speed, reduce costs, and lessen the environmental impact of transportation.

Cold Chain Technologies

The cold chain—the temperature-controlled supply chain—is critical for preserving the integrity of perishable goods. Innovations such as smart refrigeration systems, IoT sensors, and advanced insulation materials are helping to reduce spoilage during transport.

These technologies are particularly vital for developing nations, where lack of refrigeration is a major cause of food loss. Portable, solar-powered cold storage units are being deployed to rural areas to extend the shelf life of fruits, vegetables, and dairy products.

Ethical Considerations and Sustainability

With rapid innovation comes ethical complexity. The ways we grow and consume food are deeply tied to cultural, moral, and environmental values.

Animal Welfare

Lab-grown meat and plant-based alternatives raise questions about the necessity of traditional animal farming. While these technologies offer ethical advantages by eliminating animal slaughter, they may disrupt livelihoods in rural communities dependent on livestock.

There is also ongoing debate about the labelling of synthetic foods. Should lab-grown meat be marketed as "meat," or should it have a distinct classification? The answer could influence consumer perception and regulatory approaches.

Equity and Access

One of the main criticisms of food technology is its accessibility. High-tech solutions often debut in wealthy markets, potentially widening the gap between those who can afford innovation and those who cannot. There's a real risk that food tech could become a luxury for the privileged rather than a global solution.

For technology to be truly transformative, it must be scalable and accessible. Non-profits, governments, and private companies will need to work together to subsidize costs, build infrastructure, and ensure equitable distribution.

Environmental Footprint

Although many food tech innovations are marketed as sustainable, their full environmental impact is not yet known. Producing lab-grown meat, for instance, requires significant energy, much of which may come from non-renewable sources unless paired with clean energy solutions.

Vertical farms also rely heavily on electricity for lighting and climate control. To maximize their sustainability, these systems must be powered by renewable energy and optimized for efficiency.

The Battle Against Food Waste

Globally, about one-third of all food produced is wasted. This not only squanders resources but also contributes to greenhouse gas emissions. Food technology offers several solutions to this massive problem.

Smart Packaging

Intelligent packaging can extend shelf life and improve food safety. Some packaging materials change colour when food spoils, while others include QR codes that provide freshness data. This helps consumers and retailers make better decisions and reduce unnecessary disposal.

Food Redistribution Platforms

Apps and platforms like Too Good To Go, OLIO, and Karma connect restaurants and stores with surplus food to consumers willing to buy it at a discount or even receive it for free. These initiatives reduce food waste and provide affordable meals, especially in urban centres.

Upcycling Food Waste

Innovative startups are turning food waste into new products. For example, fruit peels can be transformed into biodegradable packaging, while leftover grains from breweries are repurposed into protein bars. This circular economy approach helps close the loop on food waste and resource consumption.

AI-Powered Waste Management

In commercial kitchens and supermarkets, AI sensors can analyse what gets discarded and why. This data is then used to adjust purchasing, menu planning, and pricing strategies. Companies like Winnow and Leanpath are helping the food service industry save millions of meals from the landfill each year.

Looking Ahead: Toward a Resilient Food Future

Food technology holds immense potential to reshape our food systems in ways that are sustainable, ethical, and inclusive. However, realizing this potential will require collaboration across disciplines and sectors.

Governments must craft policies that support innovation while protecting public health and ensuring equity. Companies must commit to transparency, environmental stewardship, and fair labour practices. And consumers must remain informed and engaged, making choices that align with both their values and the planet's needs.

Ultimately, feeding the future will not be about one silver-bullet technology, but about integrating diverse approaches—traditional knowledge, scientific advancement, and human compassion—to build a food system that nourishes both people and the planet.

The 21st century is witnessing a demographic shift unlike any in human history. Advances in medicine, nutrition, and living conditions have significantly extended life expectancy in many parts of the world. While this is a testament to human progress, it also brings a complex web of societal, economic, and ethical challenges. The global population of individuals aged 65 and older is projected to more than double by 2050, placing unprecedented strain on healthcare systems, economies, and social structures. At the same time, the aging population presents opportunities for innovation, community building, and redefining what it means to grow old.

Advances in Medicine and Lifespan Extension

Medical science has played a pivotal role in extending human life. Breakthroughs in pharmaceuticals, diagnostics, and preventive care have helped control chronic diseases and significantly reduce mortality rates. Today, conditions that were once fatal—such as heart disease, diabetes, and certain cancers—are increasingly manageable with early detection and continuous care.

One of the most promising areas of research in longevity science is the study of senescence, the process by which cells cease to divide and function. Scientists are exploring ways to delay or reverse cellular aging using senolytic drugs, genetic therapies, and advanced biotechnology. Telomere extension, mitochondrial repair, and CRISPR-based genome editing are just a few of the experimental strategies aimed at enhancing human longevity.

Organizations such as the SENS Research Foundation and Calico (a Google subsidiary) are heavily invested in the science of aging, with the goal not just of extending lifespan, but also of improving healthspan—the number of years a person lives in good health. This focus represents a paradigm shift: from simply living longer to living better.

Impact on Healthcare Systems and Economies

As the population ages, healthcare systems face mounting pressure. Older adults typically require more medical attention, particularly for chronic conditions, mobility issues, and cognitive decline. This growing demand risks overwhelming existing healthcare infrastructures, especially in countries with underfunded or understaffed medical services.

Long-term care facilities, geriatric specialists, and home health aides are in high demand, yet supply often falls short. Many healthcare systems are unprepared for the scale of elderly care needed in the coming decades. Policymakers are being forced to rethink funding models, including how to sustain public pension and health insurance programs as the ratio of working-age individuals to retirees declines.

Economically, the aging population presents both a burden and an opportunity. On one hand, it strains public finances and may slow economic growth due to a shrinking workforce. On the other hand, the "silver economy"—goods and services tailored to older adults—is expanding. Industries such as healthcare technology, age-friendly housing, and elder tourism are set to thrive.

Moreover, many older adults remain active contributors to the economy. From entrepreneurship to caregiving, retirees bring experience and stability. In societies that embrace intergenerational collaboration, aging populations can become assets rather than liabilities.

The Challenge of Integrating Older Generations into Society

Social integration is critical to the well-being of older individuals. Yet many face isolation, marginalization, and a loss of identity post-retirement. Urban planning, community design, and social policies must evolve to accommodate an aging population.

Age-friendly cities, a concept promoted by the World Health Organization (WHO), aim to foster environments where older adults can live safely, enjoy good health, and continue to participate fully in society. These cities prioritize accessible public spaces, transportation, housing, and services tailored to senior citizens.

Intergenerational programs, where younger and older people collaborate on community projects or live in shared housing arrangements, are gaining popularity. These initiatives help bridge generational divides, reduce loneliness, and cultivate mutual respect.

There is also a cultural shift occurring in how aging is perceived. In many Eastern cultures, elders are revered and hold respected positions within families and communities. Western societies are slowly beginning to reevaluate youth-centric narratives and recognize the wisdom, resilience, and value of older adults.

Enhancing Quality of Life for the Elderly Through Technology

Technology offers immense potential to improve the quality of life for older adults. Smart home devices, wearable health trackers, and telehealth services allow seniors to maintain independence while managing their health.

For example, fall-detection systems and AI-powered personal assistants can alert caregivers or emergency services in real-time. Medication management apps help ensure adherence to treatment plans, reducing hospital readmissions. Voice-controlled interfaces make technology more accessible for those with limited mobility or vision.

Robotics is another promising area. Companion robots like Japan's PARO seal provide emotional support and interaction for individuals with dementia. More advanced models are being developed to assist with household chores, mobility, and even physical therapy.

Virtual reality (VR) is being used in nursing homes to offer cognitive stimulation, pain management, and even "virtual travel" experiences. These innovations can combat depression and mental decline, especially in residents with limited mobility or social engagement.

Digital literacy remains a barrier for many older individuals, but this gap is narrowing. Increasing numbers of seniors are embracing smartphones, social media, and online learning platforms. Community centres, libraries, and nonprofits are offering tech training tailored to older users, helping them stay connected and informed.

The Path Forward: Rethinking Aging

Aging is not merely a medical condition to be managed—it is a life stage deserving of dignity, purpose, and engagement. Societies that plan for aging populations with foresight and compassion will be better positioned to harness the potential of their elder citizens.

This includes reforming retirement systems to allow flexible working options, encouraging life-long learning, and promoting preventative healthcare from an early age. Urban planners, architects, educators, and technologists must collaborate to build inclusive environments where people of all ages can thrive.

Research into longevity must be balanced with ethical considerations, ensuring that the benefits of medical advances are distributed fairly. The goal should not be to pursue immortality, but to create a world where extended life is accompanied by vitality, connection, and contribution.

In the coming decades, the question is not whether populations will age—it is how we respond. Will we view aging as a societal burden, or as a catalyst for innovation and empathy? The answer will shape not only the future of elder care, but the fabric of human civilization itself.

Globalization has been one of the defining forces of the late 20th and early 21st centuries. Driven by advances in transportation, communication, and technology, the world has become more interconnected than ever before. Goods, services, information, and people now move across borders with a speed and volume unimaginable in previous centuries. Yet, this surge in global interconnectedness has not been without consequence. Alongside the benefits of increased trade, cultural exchange, and innovation, there has emerged a growing backlash—manifested in the resurgence of nationalism, protectionism, and political populism.

This chapter explores the evolving dynamics between globalization and nationalism, analyzing their implications for cultural identity, economic systems, and the future of international cooperation. As we move deeper into the 21st century, understanding this tension will be crucial for navigating a world where global and local interests often appear at odds.

The Rise of Globalization

Globalization refers to the process by which national and regional economies, societies, and cultures become integrated through global networks. These include trade agreements, financial markets, digital communication platforms, multinational corporations, and migratory movements. The post-World War II period, especially from the 1990s onward, saw a dramatic acceleration in globalization. Institutions such as the World Trade Organization (WTO), International Monetary Fund (IMF), and World Bank played central roles in promoting open markets and economic liberalization.

Transnational corporations expanded their operations worldwide, capitalizing on labour markets in the Global South and tapping into new consumer bases. The internet revolution further dismantled traditional barriers, enabling instantaneous communication and digital commerce across continents. Culturally, globalization ushered in an era where ideas, fashion, food, music, and media from diverse cultures could be accessed and adopted globally. The world became a more hybrid, multicultural, and interdependent place.

The Backlash: Nationalism and Protectionism Resurge

Despite—or perhaps because of—these changes, the 21st century has seen the rise of a counter-current: a renewed emphasis on nationalism and protectionism. Economic globalization, while creating wealth, has also exacerbated inequality. Many working-class communities in industrialized nations experienced job losses due to outsourcing and automation. In developing countries, exposure to global capital often led to environmental degradation, labour exploitation, and cultural homogenization.

This disillusionment gave rise to populist political movements that critique globalization as a system that benefits the elite at the expense of ordinary citizens. Nationalist rhetoric has gained traction in various parts of the world, promoting sovereignty, traditional values, and border control over global cooperation. The election of nationalist leaders in countries like the United States, Brazil, India, and Hungary reflects this shift. Brexit, the United Kingdom's decision to leave the European Union, stands as one of the most high-profile rejections of transnational integration.

Protectionism has returned to mainstream economic discourse, with governments imposing tariffs, renegotiating trade deals, and prioritizing domestic industries. This trend has sparked fears of a new era of economic fragmentation, reminiscent of the interwar period of the 20th century.

The Cultural Tug-of-War: Identity vs. Integration

At the heart of the globalization-nationalism debate lies the issue of cultural identity. While globalization facilitates cross-cultural understanding and fusion, it can also lead to cultural dilution or loss. Local languages, traditions, and ways of life often struggle to compete with dominant global cultures, particularly Western consumerist culture.

Nationalism, in this context, is often a reaction to perceived cultural erosion. It seeks to reaffirm local values, heritage, and sovereignty in the face of globalization's homogenizing tendencies. This has led to an increase in cultural protectionism, such as quotas on foreign media content, campaigns to promote indigenous languages, and restrictions on immigration.

However, not all cultural responses to globalization are reactionary. Many societies have adopted syncretic approaches, blending global influences with local customs to create new hybrid identities. The popularity of Korean pop culture (K-pop), for instance, demonstrates how non-Western societies can project their cultural identity globally while also participating in the international cultural economy.

Balancing openness and preservation is a delicate act. Excessive cultural protectionism can lead to xenophobia and isolationism, while unchecked globalization can result in cultural erasure and societal dislocation.

Economic Shifts in a Polarized World

Economically, the tension between globalization and nationalism is playing out in complex ways. Global supply chains, once heralded as the most efficient means of production, are now being re-evaluated in light of geopolitical risks and pandemic-induced disruptions. Nations are investing in reshoring industries, securing critical supply chains, and reducing dependence on foreign entities.

China's rise as a global economic powerhouse has further complicated the landscape. The U.S.-China trade war revealed the fragility of economic interdependence when national interests clash. As a result, regional economic blocs are gaining prominence—such as the Regional Comprehensive Economic Partnership (RCEP) in Asia and strengthened trade relationships within the European Union.

Digital globalization adds another layer of complexity. Tech giants like Google, Amazon, and Facebook operate globally, but their influence raises concerns over data privacy, monopolistic practices, and the erosion of national regulatory power. Efforts to rein in these entities through digital sovereignty laws and antitrust regulations are intensifying.

Moreover, economic nationalism is fuelling debates over immigration, labour markets, and resource control. Some governments argue that protecting local jobs and industries is essential for national security and cohesion. Others warn that such policies risk economic stagnation and reduced innovation.

The Future of International Cooperation

Despite nationalist currents, the challenges facing humanity are increasingly global in nature. Climate change, pandemics, cyber threats, and international terrorism do not respect borders. Solving these problems requires unprecedented levels of cooperation, coordination, and mutual trust.

Global governance institutions, however, are under strain. The United Nations, World Health Organization, and other multilateral bodies face criticism for inefficiency, lack of representation, or bias. Reforming these institutions to reflect a more multipolar world is essential for rebuilding confidence in global cooperation.

New forms of international collaboration are also emerging. Transnational alliances on climate action, such as the Paris Agreement, represent a collective acknowledgment of shared responsibility. Scientific networks, especially during the COVID-19 pandemic, showcased how global cooperation can accelerate solutions.

Cities, corporations, and civil society organizations are playing increasingly important roles in global diplomacy. As nation-states retreat into protectionist stances, subnational and transnational actors are stepping up to fill the void, advocating for global issues from a decentralized front.

Artificial intelligence, biotechnology, and space exploration present both opportunities and challenges for global governance. As these frontiers expand, the need for international frameworks becomes more pressing. Ensuring ethical standards, equitable access, and peaceful cooperation will test humanity's capacity for unity in diversity.

Navigating the Crossroads

Globalization and nationalism are not inherently incompatible. The future lies in finding a balance—what some scholars term "cosmopolitan nationalism" or "inclusive sovereignty." This approach recognizes the legitimacy of national identity and self-determination while acknowledging our interconnected destiny.

Education plays a pivotal role in fostering this balance. Teaching global citizenship, empathy, and critical thinking can help future generations appreciate diversity without losing sight of their roots. Media and technology must also be harnessed to promote dialogue over division, cooperation over competition.

Ultimately, the question is not whether globalization or nationalism will prevail, but how they can coexist in a way that serves humanity as a whole. The task is to build societies that are resilient, inclusive, and forward-looking—capable of honouring local heritage while participating in a shared global future.

As the world navigates this tension, the decisions made by leaders, institutions, and individuals will shape not only national destinies but the trajectory of global civilization itself. The stakes are high, but so too is the potential for a more equitable, sustainable, and connected world.

Chapter 21: The Rise of Nationalism: A Response to Global Challenges?

The early 21st century has seen a sharp resurgence in nationalist sentiment across much of the globe, with movements advocating for self-determination, cultural preservation, and economic protectionism rising to political prominence. This phenomenon is not confined to a single region or ideology; it manifests in diverse ways across democracies and authoritarian states alike. Yet the common thread is the assertion of national identity and sovereignty in response to perceived threats posed by globalization, migration, and supranational institutions.

This chapter explores the resurgence of nationalism through four lenses: the nature of contemporary nationalist movements, their influence on international relations, the friction between national interests and global challenges, and potential future scenarios shaped by this ideological shift.

Contemporary Nationalist Movements

Modern nationalist movements do not emerge in a vacuum. They are responses—often reactive, sometimes proactive—to a complex web of economic, cultural, and geopolitical changes. The 21st-century global order has been shaped by rapid technological advancement, shifting demographics, widening economic disparities, and the erosion of trust in traditional political institutions. These dynamics have contributed to an identity crisis in many societies.

In Europe, nationalist parties have capitalized on economic insecurities and concerns over immigration. The National Rally in France, led by Marine Le Pen, gained momentum by positioning itself as a defender of French culture and sovereignty. In Hungary, Viktor Orbán's Fidesz party has institutionalized a model of "illiberal democracy," emphasizing Christian identity, border security, and resistance to EU influence. Italy's Brothers of Italy, under Giorgia Meloni, promotes a strong anti-immigration stance, opposing multicultural policies and framing them as threats to Italian heritage.

The Brexit referendum in the United Kingdom stands as one of the clearest expressions of nationalist backlash against supranational governance. The campaign emphasized reclaiming control over borders, laws, and trade, framing the European Union as a bureaucratic structure that undermined British sovereignty.

In the United States, nationalism took the form of "America First." Donald Trump's presidency reoriented American foreign policy away from multilateralism, imposed tariffs on key trading partners, withdrew from several international agreements, and enacted strict immigration measures. His rhetoric emphasized a nostalgic return to national greatness, often at the expense of long-standing alliances and global norms.

Outside the Western world, nationalism has gained ground in countries like India, where the ruling Bharatiya Janata Party (BJP) under Narendra Modi promotes Hindu nationalism. In Brazil, Jair Bolsonaro's government invoked national pride while rolling back environmental regulations and marginalizing indigenous voices. Turkey under Recep Tayyip Erdoğan blends religious identity with nationalist fervour, bolstering a sense of neo-Ottoman revival.

Each of these movements frames nationalism as a solution to the erosion of identity and agency in an interconnected, often chaotic world. Whether rooted in ethnicity, religion, or historical grievance, they reflect a global yearning for control, belonging, and meaning.

Impact on Global Policies and Alliances

The spread of nationalism has reshaped global alliances and diplomatic norms. One immediate consequence is the weakening of multinational institutions that have underpinned the post-WWII global order. Organizations like the European Union, NATO, and the United Nations, built on ideals of shared responsibility and collective action, have faced growing skepticism and internal divisions.

Brexit fundamentally challenged the EU's cohesion. Although it did not spark a mass exodus, it emboldened eurosceptic parties across Europe, leading to more polarized discourse around national sovereignty versus integration. The EU's response to migration, economic recovery, and pandemic management has been subject to nationalist critique, sometimes undermining coordinated action.

The United States' nationalist turn under Trump impacted multiple international frameworks. Withdrawing from the Paris Agreement on climate change, the Iran nuclear deal (JCPOA), and the Trans-Pacific Partnership signaled a retreat from cooperative governance. Trade wars with China and tariffs on allies like Canada and the EU disrupted global supply chains and reduced trust in U.S. leadership.

Nationalism has also reshaped security policy. NATO members have faced uncertainty over U.S. commitment to collective defence. At the same time, countries like Poland and Hungary have sought bilateral security arrangements while pushing back against EU rule-of-law mechanisms, viewing them as infringements on national autonomy.

In Asia, China's assertive nationalism plays a distinct role. The Chinese Communist Party (CCP) frames its governance as the restoration of historical greatness. Nationalist narratives around Taiwan, the South China Sea, and Hong Kong galvanize public support and justify territorial claims. China's Belt and Road Initiative, though presented as economic cooperation, is often seen as an instrument of geopolitical influence.

Russia's foreign policy under Vladimir Putin similarly reflects nationalist imperatives. The annexation of Crimea, intervention in Ukraine, and emphasis on protecting Russian speakers abroad are couched in nationalist rhetoric. These moves have redrawn borders, challenged international norms, and provoked military and economic responses from the West.

The combined effect of these developments is a fragmentation of global consensus. As countries prioritize national interests, collective responses to common threats become harder to organize. This trend signals a shift from liberal internationalism to a more transactional and competitive global landscape.

Tensions Between Global Issues and National Interests

The rise of nationalism poses a fundamental dilemma: the world's most pressing problems do not respect national borders. Climate change, pandemics, cyberattacks, terrorism, and economic volatility require coordinated solutions. Yet nationalist politics often prioritize short-term domestic gains over long-term global stability.

The COVID-19 pandemic offered a stark illustration. National governments rushed to secure vaccines, restrict exports, and close borders, often at the expense of global equity and transparency. Wealthier countries stockpiled medical supplies, while poorer nations struggled to access basic healthcare resources. The idea of a shared human challenge was overshadowed by competition for resources and blame-shifting.

Climate change presents an even more daunting test. It demands collective sacrifice and coordinated policy. Yet nationalist leaders frequently downplay environmental concerns, framing them as threats to economic growth or national independence. Brazil's deforestation of the Amazon, the United States' brief withdrawal from the Paris Agreement, and Australia's reluctance to curb fossil fuel exports are examples of how nationalism can hinder climate action.

In trade, nationalist protectionism disrupts global markets. The resurgence of tariffs and economic nationalism undermines supply chain efficiency and increases geopolitical risk. Policies designed to protect domestic industries often result in retaliatory measures, sparking trade disputes with broader implications.

Migration is another flashpoint. Nationalist narratives frame migrants as cultural threats or economic burdens, leading to restrictive asylum policies and border fortifications. This response ignores the global drivers of migration—conflict, poverty, and climate change—and reduces complex humanitarian issues to binary choices.

Cybersecurity and digital governance also suffer from a lack of coordinated frameworks. National governments often act unilaterally, prioritizing surveillance, censorship, or domestic tech development. As AI, data privacy, and digital warfare become central to global stability, nationalist fragmentation could delay essential global standards.

The cumulative result is a growing mismatch between the scale of our problems and the tools available to address them. Nationalism, in its current form, risks weakening the very institutions needed to manage global risks.

Future Scenarios Based on Current Political Trajectory

Looking ahead, the evolution of nationalism could lead to several distinct global futures, depending on how societies and governments navigate this ideological resurgence.

1. The Age of Fortress Nations

In this scenario, nationalism continues to intensify. Countries build walls—literal and metaphorical—to protect borders, industries, and cultures. International institutions become obsolete or toothless. Migration is criminalized, and global agreements are replaced by ad hoc bilateral deals. While this may deliver a sense of security and control in the short term, it leads to rising inequality, increased conflict, and a weakened global safety net. Collective responses to existential threats like climate change or pandemics become nearly impossible.

2. Adaptive Nationalism

A more balanced path envisions nationalism evolving into a form of resilient sovereignty. States assert their national identity but engage constructively with global systems. International cooperation is reframed not as surrendering sovereignty but as strengthening it. Countries invest in domestic capacities— like energy independence or digital infrastructure—while remaining active in reforming global governance. Multilateral institutions become more flexible, allowing for tailored cooperation that respects local contexts.

3. Supranational Rebalancing

Eventually, the limits of nationalism may become too glaring to ignore. Crises like climate migration, water scarcity, or cyberwarfare may force a new wave of globalism—one driven by pragmatism rather than ideology. Under this model, existing institutions are restructured to be more democratic, inclusive, and accountable. Regional unions may deepen cooperation, and transnational actors (cities, corporations, and NGOs) play larger roles in solving global problems.

4. Hybrid Governance Models

This scenario combines local sovereignty with global participation. States retain cultural and political autonomy while embracing decentralized global governance. Citizen-led diplomacy, open-source policymaking, and technology-driven platforms enable participation beyond traditional state actors. A polycentric world order emerges, where power is shared across levels, and legitimacy is earned through transparency and collaboration.

Final Reflections

Nationalism is a powerful force because it speaks to deep human needs: identity, belonging, control. Its rise in the 21st century reflects real discontents with globalization, inequality, and cultural erosion. But when nationalism turns inward and adversarial, it limits our ability to tackle the shared challenges that define our era.

The task is not to suppress nationalism but to channel it toward constructive ends. Civic nationalism, rooted in inclusive values and shared purpose, can coexist with global responsibility. The choice ahead is not between nationalism and globalism, but between narrow isolation and intelligent cooperation.

The shape of the future will depend on how leaders, institutions, and citizens engage with this challenge. If we can redefine sovereignty to mean stewardship—of people, resources, and the planet—we may find a path that honours national pride while building a sustainable, interconnected world.

Chapter 22: Climate Change: Technology as a Savior?

Climate change is no longer a hypothetical crisis—it's an unfolding reality. Ice caps are melting, seas are rising, weather patterns are shifting dramatically, and ecosystems are under pressure. It's a global emergency that touches every aspect of life, from agriculture and housing to migration and national security. As the crisis deepens, many turn their eyes toward science and technology for solutions. But is technology our saviour—or could it also be part of the problem?

This chapter explores the breadth of technological innovation aimed at tackling climate change, the contentious realm of geoengineering, the necessity of public and policy involvement, and the uncertain but critical future of human adaptability to increasingly severe climate extremes.

Technological Innovations Combatting Climate Change

Renewable Energy Transformation

The rapid growth of renewable energy technologies is one of the most promising developments in the climate crisis response. Solar, wind, hydro, and geothermal energy sources are now cornerstones of clean energy strategies worldwide. The cost of solar photovoltaic cells has fallen by over 80% in the past decade, making solar power accessible to countries across the economic spectrum. Wind power, particularly offshore wind, is expanding quickly in regions like Northern Europe and the U.S. East Coast.

Energy storage systems are also improving. Battery technologies—especially lithium-ion and emerging alternatives like solid-state and sodium-ion batteries—are key to managing the intermittent nature of renewables. Grid-level storage solutions are allowing for more reliable power delivery, especially during peak usage times or weather fluctuations.

Decentralized systems like microgrids and community solar initiatives are empowering local resilience. In rural Africa, small-scale solar networks are providing electricity to communities for the first time. In urban centres, building-integrated solar panels are turning skyscrapers into vertical energy harvesters.

Carbon Capture and Utilization (CCU)

Carbon Capture, Utilization, and Storage (CCUS) involves trapping carbon dioxide at the source—such as power plants and industrial sites—then either storing it underground or converting it into usable materials. The technology is gaining traction, particularly in heavy-emitting industries like cement, steel, and chemical manufacturing.

Some startups are innovating with atmospheric capture—removing CO_2 directly from the air. Climeworks in Iceland is among the pioneers using geothermal energy to power direct air capture (DAC) systems, storing CO_2 in basalt rock formations.

Utilization pathways include transforming CO_2 into carbon-neutral fuels, plastics, or building materials. These circular processes aim to reduce the environmental footprint of industrial operations and create new economies around waste-to-resource models.

Precision Agriculture and Food Systems

Agriculture contributes roughly a quarter of global greenhouse gas emissions. It also suffers immensely from climate impacts—drought, flooding, and unpredictable seasons. Precision agriculture uses sensors, GPS mapping, AI, and data analytics to optimize irrigation, fertilization, and pest control, reducing input waste and emissions.

Biotechnological advances have led to climate-resilient crop varieties—plants engineered or bred for drought resistance, salt tolerance, and heat endurance. Indoor vertical farming, aquaponics, and controlled-environment agriculture are offering alternatives to traditional land-intensive farming, reducing water usage and allowing food production closer to urban centres.

Livestock emissions—particularly methane—are being addressed through dietary supplements, like seaweed additives, that reduce emissions during digestion. Lab-grown meats and plant-based alternatives are creating protein sources with a lower carbon footprint.

Sustainable Construction and Transportation

Buildings and transportation are major sources of emissions. Greener construction materials such as carbon-negative concrete and cross-laminated timber are emerging as alternatives. Smart buildings equipped with efficient heating, lighting, and cooling systems are reducing energy consumption.

The electrification of transportation is gaining momentum. Electric vehicles (EVs) are expanding in range and affordability, supported by growing infrastructure for charging. Advances in hydrogen fuel cells are complementing battery tech, particularly for freight and industrial transport.

Public transportation is also undergoing green shifts: electric buses, high-speed trains, and shared mobility platforms are helping cities reduce reliance on fossil fuels. Urban design is playing a role too, with walkable cities, bike lanes, and integrated transit networks gaining popularity.

Controversies and Debates on Geoengineering

Geoengineering represents the most controversial set of climate technologies—large-scale interventions designed to manipulate Earth's systems to counteract global warming. These ideas push ethical, political, and scientific boundaries.

Solar Radiation Management (SRM)

SRM includes proposals to reflect a fraction of sunlight back into space, thereby reducing global temperatures. Techniques range from stratospheric aerosol injection (similar to volcanic eruptions) to marine cloud brightening or space-based reflectors.

Advocates argue these methods could offer emergency relief if warming becomes unmanageable. But the risks are immense. Changing atmospheric radiation could shift global rainfall patterns, trigger droughts, or affect the monsoon cycle. SRM doesn't address ocean acidification and could entrench reliance on fossil fuels by reducing the sense of urgency.

The political dimension is murky: who decides when and how to deploy such technology? What happens if one nation acts unilaterally? The international community has yet to establish frameworks for governing such interventions.

Carbon Dioxide Removal (CDR)

CDR techniques—ranging from afforestation and soil carbon enhancement to ocean fertilization and bioenergy with carbon capture—aim to reduce existing atmospheric CO_2.

While seen as more "natural," these strategies still face scalability, cost, and land use challenges. Large-scale tree planting can strain water supplies and compete with food production. Ocean fertilization poses risks to marine ecosystems and has unclear long-term impacts.

Moral Hazard of Technological Solutions

A core concern is that relying on geoengineering or futuristic tech may divert attention from proven but politically challenging solutions like emissions cuts, energy conservation, and sustainable living.

Technological optimism can breed complacency. If societies believe they can engineer their way out of the crisis, will they delay necessary systemic changes? The risk of false security looms large.

The Role of Policy and Public Engagement in Solutions

Technological solutions don't operate in a vacuum—they require frameworks, regulation, funding, and public trust. The interaction between science, policy, and society is crucial to ensure that innovations serve the broader public good.

Policy as a Catalyst for Innovation

Strong climate policy can drive investment and shape market behaviour. Carbon pricing—through taxes or cap-and-trade—internalizes environmental costs, making clean technologies more competitive.

Subsidies for renewable energy, green infrastructure investment, and R&D grants can accelerate breakthroughs. Governments also play a role in setting efficiency standards, regulating emissions, and phasing out harmful practices.

Legislation like the European Green Deal or the U.S. Inflation Reduction Act reflects how targeted policy can catalyse large-scale change. However, political instability and lobbying by entrenched fossil fuel interests continue to obstruct progress in many regions.

International Cooperation and Its Limits

Global agreements like the Paris Accord provide frameworks for collective action, but enforcement remains weak. Nationally Determined Contributions (NDCs) often fall short, and there's a gap between pledges and implementation.

Developing nations face particular challenges. Many lack the resources for ambitious climate action and require funding and technology transfers from wealthier nations. Failure to deliver on climate finance promises erodes trust and cooperation.

Grassroots Movements and Cultural Shifts

Public engagement plays a growing role. Movements like Extinction Rebellion, Fridays for Future, and Stop Cambo have shifted climate from a niche concern to a mass mobilization issue. Social media amplifies climate voices and holds politicians accountable.

Cultural norms are evolving. Eco-conscious lifestyles—minimalism, zero-waste, ethical consumerism—are gaining traction. But systemic change requires more than individual action. It demands collective will, institutional transformation, and sustained pressure from civil society.

Greenwashing and Corporate Responsibility

As demand for sustainability grows, so does the temptation for greenwashing. Companies exaggerate environmental claims to attract eco-conscious consumers without making meaningful changes. Clear regulations, third-party audits, and transparent metrics are needed to separate genuine efforts from marketing spin.

At the same time, businesses can be powerful allies. Supply chain decarbonization, net-zero commitments, and circular economy models are being embraced by forward-looking companies. Investor pressure through ESG (Environmental, Social, Governance) frameworks is shifting boardroom priorities.

Predictions for Adaptability to Climate Extremes

Despite mitigation efforts, climate extremes will intensify. Adaptation is no longer optional—it's a survival strategy.

Resilient Infrastructure and Urban Planning

Cities are at the forefront of climate impacts and solutions. Heatwaves, flooding, and resource scarcity will require urban resilience. That includes heat-resistant building materials, expanded green spaces, stormwater systems, and modular housing that can withstand extreme events.

Infrastructure investment must prioritize not just durability but flexibility. Climate-responsive zoning, energy-efficient retrofits, and climate-conscious public works can reduce risk and support long-term sustainability.

Migration and Climate Displacement

Climate-driven migration is accelerating. Rising sea levels, desertification, and resource scarcity are displacing communities across Africa, Asia, and the Pacific By 2050, hundreds of millions could become climate refugees.

This will reshape geopolitics, strain humanitarian systems, and require international coordination. Border policies, asylum laws, and urban planning must adapt to absorb new populations while avoiding xenophobia and marginalization.

Behavioural and Psychological Adaptation

Beyond physical changes, societies must adapt behaviourally and psychologically. Acceptance of uncertainty, willingness to change consumption habits, and preparedness for disruption will define resilience.

Education is central—climate literacy empowers people to make informed decisions. Media, arts, and storytelling help shape cultural narratives that support long-term shifts.

Equity and Technological Access

A key risk is uneven access to climate tech. Wealthier countries and corporations may adapt quickly, while vulnerable populations are left behind. Bridging this divide requires intentional strategies: tech sharing, funding mechanisms, inclusive design, and a justice-centred approach to innovation.

The digital age has transformed nearly every aspect of our lives, from how we work and learn to how we connect and unwind. Alongside these changes, mental health has come to the forefront as a pressing public concern. Anxiety, depression, burnout, and loneliness have spiked in tandem with our rising screen time and the growing role of technology in daily life. At the same time, innovations in digital health tools offer new possibilities for support and intervention.

This chapter explores the dual nature of technology's impact on mental health: its capacity to both harm and heal. We'll look at the psychological effects of digital life, the rise of digital therapy, the potential downsides of overreliance on tech, and the broader societal efforts to address mental health crises.

The Impact of Technology on Mental Well-Being

The Pressure of Constant Connectivity

Smartphones, social media, and instant messaging have made it nearly impossible to unplug. Notifications follow us from bedroom to workplace, interrupting rest and attention. This hyperconnectivity contributes to stress, sleep disorders, and a loss of clear boundaries between work and personal life.

Studies show that constant digital interaction can cause "technostress," a type of psychological strain stemming from the expectation of immediate response and performance. Over time, this erodes concentration, increases irritability, and can contribute to long-term anxiety disorders.

Social Media and Self-Image

Social platforms can amplify feelings of inadequacy, loneliness, and social comparison. The curated highlight reels of others' lives can distort perceptions of reality, especially among teenagers and young adults. Body image issues, cyberbullying, and the addictive design of social apps deepen these problems.

Research links heavy social media use with higher rates of depression and anxiety. While these platforms offer opportunities for connection, they can also foster echo chambers, tribalism, and a constant sense of needing to measure up.

Gamification and Dopamine Loops

Apps and games are designed to trigger dopamine responses—short bursts of reward that reinforce usage. This feedback loop can become addictive. Whether it's scrolling endlessly or chasing digital achievements, the pursuit of micro-rewards can replace real-world satisfaction, leading to emotional numbness or increased anxiety when offline.

The Rise in Digital Therapy and Mental Health Apps

Accessible and Scalable Support

One of the most promising trends is the rise of digital mental health tools. Online therapy platforms like BetterHelp and Talkspace offer remote sessions with licensed therapists, increasing access for those who face geographic, financial, or scheduling barriers.

Apps such as Headspace, Calm, and Insight Timer provide guided meditations, stress management exercises, and sleep aids. Cognitive Behavioural Therapy (CBT) techniques have been digitized, allowing users to engage with mental health strategies anytime, anywhere.

AI and Chat-Based Therapy

Artificial Intelligence is being used to simulate therapeutic conversations. AI-driven bots like Woebot or Wysa offer 24/7 support, mood tracking, and evidence-based coping mechanisms. While not a substitute for human connection, these tools can offer immediate relief and early intervention.

However, critics caution against overreliance on AI for complex psychological needs. The nuance of human emotion and trauma is often beyond the scope of machine learning, raising questions about safety and effectiveness.

Digital Platforms for Community Support

Forums, group chats, and peer support networks have flourished online. Spaces like Reddit's r/depression or Discord mental health servers allow users to share experiences, coping strategies, and a sense of solidarity.

While these can offer meaningful connection, moderation and misinformation remain challenges. Not all advice is helpful, and vulnerable individuals may be exposed to harmful or triggering content.

Potential for Technology to Exacerbate Mental Health Issues

The "Always-On" Work Culture

Remote work, facilitated by digital tools, has blurred the line between home and office. Many feel the need to be available at all times, contributing to burnout and emotional fatigue. Notifications invade leisure time, and digital presenteeism—the pressure to show activity even when productivity is low—can distort work-life balance.

Surveillance and Privacy Concerns

Tracking mental health through wearables or apps raises questions about data security and surveillance. Who owns this data? Can it be used against someone in employment or insurance decisions? The ethics of mental health data are still being debated.

The Algorithmic Trap

Social media algorithms prioritize content that drives engagement, often favouring outrage, fear, or sensationalism. This can worsen anxiety and polarization. Doomscrolling—compulsively consuming negative news—has become a recognized behavioural pattern tied to mental exhaustion.

Isolation in a Hyperconnected World

Despite the abundance of communication tools, loneliness is at record levels. Virtual interactions often lack the depth and empathy of in-person relationships. For many, especially the elderly and the socially marginalized, the shift to digital-first living has intensified feelings of isolation.

Societal Responses to Mental Health Crises

Mental Health in Policy and Education

Governments and institutions are beginning to take mental health more seriously. School curricula are incorporating emotional literacy, mindfulness practices, and resilience training. Workplace wellness programs are expanding beyond fitness perks to include psychological support, mental health days, and therapy subsidies.

Public health campaigns aim to destigmatize mental illness and encourage people to seek help. Initiatives like "Time to Talk" in the UK or "Mental Health First Aid" programs globally are training people to recognize signs of distress and provide early support.

Corporate and Platform Responsibility

Tech companies are under growing pressure to address the mental health impact of their products. Some platforms have introduced screen time trackers, mental health resources, and digital well-being dashboards. Others have taken steps to limit harmful content, such as Instagram hiding likes or TikTok prompting breaks.

Still, many critics argue these changes are cosmetic and driven by PR rather than genuine concern. Real reform may require regulation—mandating ethical design, age-appropriate features, and transparent algorithms.

Community and Cultural Shifts

The stigma around mental health is slowly eroding. Celebrities, athletes, and public figures are speaking openly about their struggles, helping normalize mental health conversations. Peer networks, local support groups, and intergenerational dialogue are helping rebuild communal resilience.

There's also a growing movement toward "digital minimalism"—intentional technology use that prioritizes mental clarity and meaningful connection. Practices like digital detoxes, offline weekends, or setting device boundaries are gaining traction.

Final Thoughts

Technology is neither villain nor hero—it is a mirror of human priorities. The digital tools we've built have immense potential to support mental well-being, but they can also deepen existing fractures.

The key lies in conscious design, responsible usage, and cultural awareness. As we navigate the complexities of mental health in a wired world, we must remember that empathy, connection, and balance remain at the heart of well-being.

The challenge for the future is not to reject technology, but to humanize it—to shape digital environments that nourish the mind as much as they engage it.

Entertainment is a mirror of human desire—sometimes reflecting our dreams, sometimes shielding us from our realities. As technology has evolved, so has entertainment. What began as oral storytelling and symbolic cave art has become immersive digital worlds, endless streaming platforms, and algorithm-curated content. With every shift in medium, we've redefined how we interact with stories, art, music, and each other. But this evolution also raises a critical question: are we using entertainment to escape from life, or to understand it more deeply?

Evolution of Entertainment Mediums Through Technology

The history of entertainment is inseparable from the history of human innovation. From the invention of the printing press to the emergence of cinema, each new medium reshaped cultural narratives and expanded access to creative expression.

Radio brought music and storytelling into people's homes, forging shared cultural experiences. Television introduced serialized dramas and live news, becoming a central household fixture. With the internet, entertainment went mobile, interactive, and hyper-personalized.

Gaming evolved from arcades to online multiplayer universes, while music shifted from vinyl and cassette tapes to digital libraries and algorithm-driven playlists. Virtual reality (VR), augmented reality (AR), and AI-generated content are the latest frontiers, dissolving the boundaries between audience and creator. Now, a teenager with a phone can generate content that reaches millions.

But this democratization of media has come with a cost: a flood of content that competes for attention, often designed for maximum engagement rather than meaning.

Escapism vs. Education: Entertainment's Dual Role

At its core, entertainment offers two intertwined experiences: escapism and consciousness. Escapism provides relief—a way to disconnect from stress, pain, or monotony. Consciousness, on the other hand, arises when entertainment provokes thought, challenges perception, or fosters empathy.

Science fiction can be both a thrilling escape and a platform for societal critique. Comedies might distract us from hardship, but satire can also highlight the absurdities of power. Music might soothe the mind, or call attention to injustice. These dualities coexist in every form.

Streaming platforms know this well. Algorithms tailor content to our moods and past preferences, often reinforcing comfort zones. But among the endless scrolling, there are works that cut through—films that explore existential dread, games that simulate moral dilemmas, and art that documents climate collapse.

The entertainment industry doesn't just reflect culture; it shapes it. The stories we absorb influence how we see others, how we vote, and even how we dream. A documentary can shift public opinion. A viral TikTok trend can redefine beauty norms. A single film can humanize a distant conflict.

Content Consumption and Changing Public Consciousness

In a world saturated with content, our relationship with entertainment has become more passive and more influential. Binge-watching entire seasons has normalized addictive viewing patterns. Doomscrolling through social media blurs the line between news and spectacle. The attention economy rewards speed and emotion over nuance and reflection.

This shift affects our collective psyche. Short-form content teaches us to expect instant gratification and to avoid boredom at all costs. Complex topics are flattened into shareable clips, and moral conversations are often reduced to black-and-white narratives.

Yet, there's a counter current—people seeking meaning over distraction. Podcasts, longform essays, and slow cinema have found dedicated audiences who crave depth. Platforms like YouTube and Patreon have enabled creators to sustain thoughtful, niche work outside the demands of mainstream production.

What we choose to consume matters. Studies show that repeated exposure to violence, fear, or glamour can influence behaviour, attitudes, and emotional resilience. Equally, uplifting or challenging content can expand empathy, critical thinking, and social awareness.

Creative Expression in a Digital Age

Technology has unlocked unprecedented creative freedom. Anyone with a smartphone can record a song, make a short film, or write a novel. AI tools assist with animation, voice generation, and music composition, lowering the barrier to entry while raising philosophical questions about authorship and authenticity.

Digital platforms have also enabled marginalized voices to bypass traditional gatekeepers. Stories once excluded from mainstream media now find homes in indie games, zines, web series, and self-published books. Communities form around shared identities and narratives, strengthening cultural representation.

However, the pressure to create "engaging" content—measured in likes, shares, and monetization—can skew artistic intention. Creators must balance authenticity with algorithmic visibility, often sacrificing originality to chase virality.

As entertainment becomes more immersive—with the rise of VR concerts, AI avatars, and interactive narratives—we must question the ethics of hyperrealism. When digital experiences become indistinguishable from physical ones, how do we preserve emotional integrity and psychological well-being?

Looking Forward: A Conscious Choice

The future of entertainment depends on our collective choices. We can allow technology to reduce art to distraction—or use it to illuminate the human condition. We can feed algorithms with our basest impulses—or demand work that challenges, questions, and heals.

Education systems should integrate media literacy alongside traditional subjects. Children need to understand not just how to consume content, but how to analyse it—how to spot manipulation, recognize emotional triggers, and choose narratives that enrich rather than numb.

Policymakers and platform designers also have a role. Ethical frameworks for content curation, mental health considerations in app design, and fair compensation models for creators are essential steps toward a healthier media landscape.

At the individual level, cultivating conscious consumption is key. Ask why a particular film moved you—or why a video left you anxious. Be aware of the dopamine loops behind your viewing habits. Seek out stories that reflect not just what you want to escape from, but what you hope to understand.

Final Thoughts

Entertainment will always be a refuge and a mirror. The challenge of the digital age is to ensure it doesn't become a cage. In a world of limitless content, meaning is a choice. We can scroll endlessly through empty pixels—or pause to engage with work that speaks to our deeper selves.

In the end, the question isn't whether entertainment is good or bad. It's whether we're awake while experiencing it.

Chapter 25: Ethics of Technology: Morality in the Machine Age

As we accelerate deeper into a technological era, the ethical implications of our innovations grow increasingly complex. From artificial intelligence and biotechnology to surveillance systems and autonomous weapons, the machines we create are reshaping the fabric of human life. But with power comes responsibility. What happens when a piece of code decides who gets a loan, a diagnosis, or a jail sentence? When a drone makes a life-or-death decision? Or when a social media algorithm reinforces discrimination?

This chapter explores the ethical quandaries born in the machine age, the concept of responsible innovation, the role of society in defining ethical norms, and the difficulties of constructing universal ethical frameworks that apply across cultures, ideologies, and technologies.

The Ethical Quandaries of Technological Advancement

Autonomy and Responsibility

One of the defining traits of modern technology is autonomy. Algorithms now make decisions with minimal human oversight. In fields like finance, law enforcement, and healthcare, AI systems are increasingly used to predict outcomes and guide actions. But when these systems go wrong, accountability becomes murky. Who is to blame—the developer, the company, the machine?

Self-driving cars, for instance, pose a challenge to existing legal and moral systems. In the case of an unavoidable crash, how should a vehicle decide between harming a pedestrian or its passengers? These are not just technical problems; they are deeply philosophical.

Bias in Algorithms

Technology is not neutral. Algorithms reflect the values and biases of their creators—and the data they are trained on. Facial recognition systems have been shown to misidentify people of colour at much higher rates. Predictive policing tools often target already over-surveilled communities, reinforcing systemic injustice.

Ethical concerns also arise in hiring algorithms, educational assessments, and credit scoring systems. These tools, if not carefully regulated, can codify discrimination under the guise of objectivity.

Surveillance and Consent

The rise of surveillance capitalism—where companies harvest personal data to predict and influence behaviour—raises profound ethical questions. From smartphone tracking to facial recognition in public spaces, our movements, preferences, and private lives are increasingly exposed.

Consent, in this context, is often meaningless. Most users do not fully understand the terms they agree to, and opting out is rarely a viable option. This undermines personal autonomy and opens the door to manipulation.

Manipulation and Autonomy

Digital platforms are designed to keep us engaged, often by exploiting psychological vulnerabilities. Algorithms feed us content that reinforces existing beliefs and emotional reactions. This not only polarizes societies but also challenges the notion of free will. Are we truly making choices, or are we being nudged, primed, and persuaded by unseen forces?

Manipulation at scale—through algorithmic curation, deepfakes, and psychographic targeting—can undermine democracy itself. The Cambridge Analytica scandal is just one example of how data-driven persuasion can distort elections and public opinion.

Responsible Innovation: Balancing Progress with Morality

Ethics by Design

To create a future aligned with human values, ethics must be embedded in the design process—not tacked on afterward. This means involving ethicists, sociologists, and diverse communities in the development of new technologies.

Human-centred design encourages developers to consider the impact of their work on people's rights, dignity, and well-being. Ethical review boards, impact assessments, and stakeholder consultations are steps toward ensuring that innovation does not outpace moral responsibility.

Regulation and Oversight

Laws often lag behind technology. As a result, many innovations operate in regulatory grey zones. From AI-generated art to brain-computer interfaces, new inventions raise questions that existing laws were never meant to answer.

There is a growing call for proactive regulation. The European Union's AI Act is one example—aiming to classify and regulate AI systems based on risk. But global coordination is lacking, and tech giants often lobby against restrictive measures.

Striking the right balance between fostering innovation and protecting society is an ongoing challenge. Overregulation can stifle creativity, while under regulation can lead to harm.

Corporate Responsibility

Tech companies wield immense influence but often prioritize profit over principle. Corporate ethics policies and "responsible AI" initiatives are a start, but self-regulation has clear limits. Voluntary codes of conduct lack enforceability, and ethical commitments can be undermined by market pressures.

Public pressure, whistleblowers, and activist shareholders have sometimes pushed companies toward better behaviour. But without structural accountability, ethical lapses will remain common.

The Role of Society in Shaping Ethical Standards

Public Discourse and Awareness

Ethical decisions should not be left solely to engineers, executives, or policymakers. A democratic society must foster public debate about the direction of technological progress. Citizens need to be informed, engaged, and empowered to influence how technologies are used.

Media, education, and community forums all play a role in shaping ethical awareness. People must understand not just how technology works, but what it means—socially, politically, and philosophically.

Education and Critical Thinking

Ethical literacy should be a core part of education systems. This includes teaching students how to question technological narratives, recognize bias, and evaluate consequences.

Interdisciplinary education—combining computer science with philosophy, sociology, and psychology—can prepare future technologists to think beyond code. It can also help citizens become more thoughtful consumers and participants in the tech ecosystem.

Cultural and Generational Differences

What counts as ethical varies widely across cultures. A surveillance tool seen as invasive in one country might be accepted as a safety measure in another. Generational gaps also influence perspectives—older generations may value privacy differently than digital natives.

Developing ethical frameworks that respect pluralism while upholding basic human rights is a delicate task. Ethical universals may be aspirational, but sensitivity to context is essential.

The Challenge of Universal Ethical Frameworks

Relativity vs. Universality

Some argue that ethics are culturally constructed and should not be imposed universally. Others believe certain rights and values—like dignity, autonomy, and justice—should be upheld globally.

This tension plays out in international debates about internet freedom, data sovereignty, and AI governance. Creating ethical guidelines that are both principled and adaptable is one of the biggest challenges of our time.

Techno-Ethics and the Future

As we approach the age of artificial general intelligence, brain-computer interfaces, and synthetic life, ethical considerations will become even more complex. What rights do sentient machines have? Should we engineer morality into robots? Who decides what constitutes a "good" algorithm?

The future will likely involve ethical dilemmas we haven't yet imagined. Preparing for them means cultivating a moral imagination now—asking not just what we can build, but whether we should.

Final Thoughts

Technology does not create ethics—it reveals them. It magnifies our values, our priorities, and our blind spots. As we build more powerful tools, we must also build stronger moral foundations.

The ethics of technology is not a fixed rulebook—it is a living conversation, shaped by choices, consequences, and collective reflection. In the machine age, humanity's greatest task is to ensure that the tools we create serve not just our capabilities, but our conscience.

The machines are learning. Are we?

Chapter 26: Work and Leisure: The Future of Employment

The nature of work has always been subject to change, but the digital revolution and acceleration of automation have brought the future of employment into sharper, more urgent focus. What we once thought of as stable careers are becoming obsolete. Entire industries are shifting, and a growing number of jobs are performed not by humans but by algorithms, machines, or AI systems. At the same time, the concept of leisure is transforming, often blending into work as boundaries dissolve.

This chapter explores the fundamental shifts in how we define, pursue, and experience work and leisure, asking what it means to live a meaningful life in an age when employment is no longer guaranteed, and where the traditional 9-to-5 model may soon be a relic of the past.

Shifts in the Nature of Work Due to Technology

Work is evolving beyond offices, factory floors, and service counters. Remote work, gig platforms, digital nomadism, and AI-enhanced productivity tools have fragmented the idea of a traditional workplace. What used to require physical presence now often needs only a stable internet connection.

Automation is replacing repetitive, rules-based tasks at scale. Clerical work, customer service, logistics, and manufacturing have all undergone digital disruption. AI can now generate reports, code software, write content, and even participate in medical diagnosis. Robotic systems manage warehouses, assist in surgeries, and perform deliveries. This rapid expansion in capability raises difficult questions: Where does human labour still hold value? And who benefits from increased efficiency—workers, or corporations?

Digital platforms like Uber, Fiverr, and Upwork have reshaped labour into task-based engagement, reducing job security and benefits while increasing flexibility. Many celebrate the autonomy these platforms offer, but they also expose workers to market volatility, algorithmic control, and lack of institutional protection.

The rise of hybrid and remote work post-pandemic has changed expectations. Workers demand more autonomy, less commuting, and meaningful tasks. But it's also created new stressors—digital surveillance, blurred boundaries, and a culture of constant availability. Technology gives us the tools to reshape work, but it doesn't decide the shape we choose.

Balancing Work-Life Integration in the Digital World

The concept of work-life balance is being replaced by work-life integration. In a hyperconnected world, work spills into home life, leisure time, and even sleep patterns. Email notifications buzz during dinner. Team meetings happen across time zones. The home becomes an office, a studio, and a site of unpaid domestic labour.

This integration has complex consequences. On one hand, it allows flexibility—parents can attend school events without losing income, freelancers can choose their hours. On the other, it dilutes rest and recovery. Without physical separation, it becomes harder to mentally disconnect from professional responsibilities.

Digital burnout is a growing problem. The pressure to be productive, always reachable, always improving, creates a cycle of anxiety and exhaustion. Self-care becomes a scheduled task rather than an organic break. Leisure turns into performance—gym sessions logged, hobbies monetized, moments curated for social validation.

Reclaiming boundaries requires more than individual discipline. Employers must adopt sustainable practices—respecting off-hours, offering mental health support, and valuing output over screen time. Societies need to reimagine what a healthy relationship with work looks like in the 21st century.

The Rise of Automation and the Redefinition of Roles

Automation isn't just replacing jobs—it's changing what jobs *are*. AI and robotics don't always eliminate roles outright; they often augment them, shifting responsibilities and requiring new skills. A marketing team may use AI to analyse data, but human creativity still drives campaign strategy. A construction worker might use drones and 3D printers, but problem-solving and adaptability remain human strengths.

What we are seeing is a shift from labour to knowledge, and from routine to adaptability. Emotional intelligence, critical thinking, and ethical judgment become more important as machines take over rote tasks. But the transition is uneven. Not everyone has access to retraining. Many workers are left behind, unable to pivot into the "jobs of the future."

Universal Basic Income (UBI) and similar concepts have emerged as potential buffers. If machines can do the work, why not decouple survival from employment? Critics argue this disincentivizes ambition. Supporters see it as a chance to unlock creativity, caregiving, and community service—forms of labour undervalued by traditional economies.

The future workforce may also include hybrid AI-human roles. A teacher might work alongside a virtual assistant. A therapist could use data-driven tools to personalize care. The key question is: will automation serve human dignity, or will it deepen inequality?

Future Possibilities for Meaningful Engagement in Work

As traditional employment structures erode, people are beginning to ask a deeper question: If I didn't have to work to survive, what would I do with my time? This shift opens space for reimagining purpose.

Some will explore the arts, science, and innovation, freed from financial constraints. Others may turn to volunteering, mentorship, or civic engagement. Work doesn't have to mean income generation—it can mean contribution, growth, or expression. In this context, leisure is no longer the opposite of work, but a different kind of meaningful activity.

Education systems must adapt. Rather than preparing students for fixed careers, we should cultivate curiosity, flexibility, and lifelong learning. Teaching people how to learn, unlearn, and adapt becomes more valuable than technical specialization alone.

New models of cooperative work—community projects, open-source platforms, time banking—may gain traction as people seek meaning beyond profit. The digital realm offers potential here: decentralized networks, blockchain-enabled economies, and global knowledge sharing.

But meaningful engagement doesn't happen automatically. It requires structures that support exploration without fear—universal healthcare, accessible education, housing stability, and a cultural shift away from productivity as the sole measure of worth.

Final Thoughts

Work is not vanishing—it's transforming. The challenge is to ensure that transformation enhances, rather than erodes, human dignity and social cohesion. As automation and AI reshape our economies, we must rethink what it means to labour, to rest, and to live well.

We need to ask better questions. Not just "What do you do for a living?" but "What do you care about?" Not just "How can you earn more?" but "How can you contribute?" The future of employment is uncertain, but the future of purpose is wide open.

The task ahead is not to fight against change, but to guide it—toward systems that prioritize well-being, equity, and human potential. In a world where machines handle the necessary, we are free to pursue the meaningful.

Culture is not static—it evolves, sometimes gradually, sometimes through sudden rupture. Technological progress, political upheaval, and global crises have historically served as catalysts for major cultural shifts. In the present era, rapid technological advancement and interconnected digital networks are transforming how culture is produced, shared, and experienced. The question is no longer whether culture is changing, but whether that change is pointing us toward a new renaissance or into a period of fragmentation and decline.

The Impact of Technology on Culture and Arts

Technology has radically reshaped how we create, distribute, and engage with cultural content. From AI-generated music and art to NFTs redefining ownership, the creative industries are undergoing a major transformation. Tools once available only to professionals are now accessible to anyone with a smartphone. This democratization has opened the floodgates of expression— but also flooded the market with content, making it harder to find quality amid the noise.

AI-generated art, for example, challenges traditional notions of creativity. Can something generated by an algorithm possess artistic value? The answer often depends on who is asking. For some, these works are valid forms of expression—art directed by human intent, shaped by machine precision. For others, they represent the hollowing out of soul in creative labor.

Music production, filmmaking, and writing have also seen shifts. Artists now work with software collaborators, automating complex tasks like mastering audio or editing footage. While this enhances productivity, it also raises questions about authenticity. Is a novel written with AI co-authorship still an authentic reflection of human experience? Or are we drifting into a space where culture becomes a commodity mass-produced by neural networks?

The line between creator and consumer is also blurring. Remix culture, memes, and user-generated content redefine participation. Fans become co-creators. Platforms like TikTok encourage reinterpretation, where a viral trend might include thousands of iterations across the globe. Creativity becomes modular— pieces borrowed, rebuilt, and shared.

Globalization vs. Localization in Cultural Expression

Globalization has allowed for a near-instantaneous exchange of ideas, styles, and values across cultures. On one hand, this fosters diversity and cross-cultural understanding. On the other, it can flatten distinctiveness, leading to homogenization where local traditions are diluted or lost.

Consider how American pop culture permeates globally—TV, music, fashion, and even political discourse. While some embrace this as a sign of global connectivity, others see it as cultural imperialism, eroding regional identities. Languages die, customs fade, and unique worldviews vanish in the pursuit of global relevance.

But localization persists. In response to global saturation, there is a resurgence of interest in indigenous art, folk traditions, and linguistic preservation. Digital platforms have ironically made it easier to maintain local identities—artists from remote areas can now reach global audiences without diluting their roots.

Hybrid identities emerge. A musician might blend traditional rhythms from West Africa with trap beats from Atlanta. A filmmaker could weave Chinese myth with cyberpunk aesthetics. This isn't the death of culture, but its recombination—a collage of influences adapted to modern sensibilities.

Yet power dynamics matter. Whose culture gets amplified? Whose voices dominate platforms? Often, those with economic and technological power control the narrative, while others struggle to be seen. The challenge is to ensure that digital globalization doesn't result in cultural monoculture, but in genuine pluralism.

Predictions on the Evolution of Creativity and Innovation

The tools of creativity are evolving, and so is our relationship with them. In the near future, we may see more collaboration between humans and machines, where artists use AI not as a replacement but as a partner. Generative design, neural style transfer, and algorithmic composition could lead to entirely new art forms.

Education systems might shift to focus less on rote learning and more on creative thinking, interdisciplinary exploration, and ethical use of technology.

Students could learn coding alongside composition, machine learning alongside music theory. As access increases, so does potential.

Virtual and augmented reality will likely play larger roles in immersive storytelling. Interactive theatre, virtual concerts, and AI-powered narrative experiences may redefine how we engage with cultural products. What we consider "art" will stretch and morph—anchored less in medium and more in experience.

But with this evolution comes risk. The commodification of creativity, driven by algorithms prioritizing engagement over substance, could stifle experimentation. Artists may tailor work to trends and analytics rather than genuine expression. The tyranny of the algorithm can lead to formulaic repetition, crowding out slow, subtle, or challenging work.

To avoid this, we'll need structures that support independent voices and cultivate curiosity. That might mean rethinking intellectual property laws to encourage creative borrowing while protecting original voices. Or designing platforms that reward depth over virality.

The Potential for a New Cultural Renaissance

Despite the challenges, there is genuine potential for a new cultural renaissance. Much like the historical Renaissance, which arose out of crisis and rediscovery, our current era presents both peril and possibility.

We have access to more knowledge, tools, and connections than any previous generation. The barriers to entry in creative fields are lower than ever. A teenager in a rural village can upload a song, sell digital art, or publish a story that reaches millions. Innovation can come from anywhere.

Movements for social justice, climate awareness, and mental health are reshaping the stories we tell. Culture is becoming more reflective, inclusive, and self-aware. Marginalized voices are gaining platforms. There's a hunger for authenticity and depth—a counter current to the shallow churn of mass content.

Communities are forming around shared values rather than geographic proximity. A writer in Seoul, a dancer in Lagos, and a game designer in São Paulo might collaborate on a project without ever meeting in person. This global web of creativity mirrors the interconnectedness of our problems—and our potential solutions.

But a renaissance is not automatic. It requires intention, support, and vision. Governments, institutions, and platforms must invest in arts education, independent media, and public cultural spaces. We must resist the commodification of culture and foster spaces for slow, unprofitable, and experimental work.

We also need a renewed sense of cultural stewardship—recognizing that culture is not just entertainment, but a lens through which we understand ourselves and each other. Artists, curators, teachers, and thinkers will play a vital role in guiding this new era.

Final Thoughts

Are we heading toward a new renaissance or a cultural decline? The answer may depend on what we choose to value. Technology can fragment or connect, amplify or distort, flatten or enrich. The tools are neutral. The outcomes are not.

Culture will continue to evolve, but the direction it takes will be shaped by our collective choices—how we educate, what we fund, whose voices we elevate, and what stories we choose to tell. We stand at a threshold. Whether we step into darkness or discovery is up to us.

The concept of community has long served as the cornerstone of human civilisation. Whether in tightly-knit villages or sprawling urban neighbourhoods, people have historically found identity, support, and purpose within social structures. But with the rapid rise of digital communication and global connectivity, the foundations of traditional community life are shifting. From message boards to metaverses, the digital age is redefining what it means to belong.

This chapter explores the transformation of social structures in a hyperconnected world. It examines how technology is reshaping engagement, identity, and relationships—and asks what community might look like in the future.

Changes in Community Engagement and Structures Due to Tech

Community used to be rooted in geography. Proximity determined friendships, business ties, religious affiliation, and even political alliances. Physical space created context—parks, schools, places of worship, and public squares served as anchors for social life. But now, digital platforms enable people to gather based on shared interest rather than shared location.

Facebook groups, Reddit threads, Discord servers, and niche forums provide spaces for people to engage deeply with others they may never meet in person. Gaming communities, wellness subcultures, and fandom networks thrive across borders. A teenager in Lagos can bond with someone in Tokyo over a shared love of animation or philosophy, all without leaving their home.

This shift has dismantled barriers. Marginalised individuals, once isolated in physical communities, can now find kinship and solidarity online. Movements like #MeToo or Black Lives Matter have leveraged digital tools to mobilise across continents. Identity-based communities—LGBTQ+, neurodivergent, or chronically ill groups—have found mutual support and validation in online spaces that may not exist offline.

But digital community is not without limitations. Algorithms shape interactions. Echo chambers emerge. Platform design can prioritise virality over empathy. The speed of digital life often sacrifices depth for immediacy. And while the internet offers vast networks, it may not always satisfy the human need for embodied connection.

Digital Communities vs. Traditional Social Networks

Digital communities function differently from traditional social networks. In analogue spaces, relationships evolve gradually through shared experiences—school runs, workplace chats, volunteer events. In contrast, digital relationships can form instantly around content, opinions, or interests. They're often transactional and transient.

Traditional communities tend to foster interdependence. You might borrow sugar from a neighbour, attend a funeral, or join a community garden. These exchanges build a sense of shared fate. Online, relationships are more modular. You might follow someone for their memes, then unfollow when their views shift. Emotional investment can be shallow, and bonds dissolve easily.

Yet digital platforms also enable new forms of intimacy. Some online friendships are deeper than those in physical proximity, forged through late-night chats, shared struggles, or collaborative projects. Virtual spaces allow people to present curated or vulnerable versions of themselves, sometimes leading to profound connections.

However, many digital platforms are profit-driven, designing interactions around engagement metrics. This can skew community dynamics, encouraging performativity over authenticity, or outrage over understanding. Community becomes content, and belonging is gamified through likes, shares, and followers.

To move forward, we need to ask: How can we design digital spaces that nurture genuine community, not just interaction? What does trust look like online? And how can digital and physical communities complement rather than replace one another?

Impact on Social Behaviour and Relationships

The digital transformation of social life has reshaped behaviour. Attention spans are shorter. Social comparison is constant. The boundary between public and private has eroded. People curate their lives for visibility, even as they struggle with loneliness behind the screen.

Younger generations, raised on social media, often experience identity development in public. Likes and comments become proxies for approval. Peer pressure migrates from hallways to timelines. While this visibility can empower marginalised voices, it also invites surveillance and self-censorship.

Online interactions can foster empathy—but also cruelty. Anonymity lowers inhibitions, leading to trolling, harassment, or misinformation. At the same time, digital platforms have enabled large-scale collective actions: crowdfunding for crises, mutual aid networks, and activist campaigns that transcend geography.

Romantic relationships are also shifting. Dating apps have transformed courtship into swiping. Long-distance relationships now thrive with the help of video calls and shared digital spaces. Families stay in touch across continents. Friendships are maintained through voice notes, memes, and multiplayer games.

Yet the quality of connection varies. Many report a paradox: being always connected but rarely seen. Physical presence carries nuances that screens can't replicate—body language, silence, and shared physical environments. As we invest more time online, it's worth asking what we may be leaving behind.

Future Predictions for Belonging in a Digital Age

The future of community will likely be hybrid. Physical and digital spaces will intertwine. Local community centres may offer virtual hubs. Digital towns might host real-life meetups. The boundary between online and offline will blur further with the expansion of augmented and virtual reality.

Metaverse platforms, still in their early stages, promise immersive social experiences. These spaces could simulate presence, allow creative expression, and host events from concerts to town halls. But they also raise questions about governance, identity, and accessibility. Who controls these digital commons?

How are norms established? And who is excluded by paywalls or tech limitations?

Blockchain and decentralised technologies may offer alternatives to platform monopolies. Peer-to-peer networks, community-owned platforms, and open-source tools could foster more democratic and resilient communities. Local digital currencies and cooperative governance models are emerging as experiments in post-capitalist social structures.

Education, too, may become a site of hybrid community. Virtual classrooms could connect students globally while local hubs support embodied learning. Mutual aid groups may evolve into long-term digital cooperatives. Even neighbourhoods may be revitalised through digital tools—apps that foster sharing, alert systems for vulnerable residents, or forums for civic participation.

The desire for belonging won't disappear. But its forms will diversify. Instead of one community, people may belong to many: one for support, another for identity, another for play or purpose. What matters is whether these communities foster dignity, connection, and mutual care—or merely simulate them.

Final Thoughts

We are in a transitional era. The digital world offers unprecedented opportunities for connection, but also introduces new complexities and risks. As our social structures evolve, we must stay mindful of what we gain and what we lose.

Community is not just about being connected—it's about being known, valued, and supported. Technology can enable this, but only if we design it with care. As we build the future, we must ensure that our digital spaces reflect the values of equity, empathy, and inclusion.

The challenge ahead is not to recreate traditional communities in digital form, but to imagine new kinds of belonging that meet the needs of a fragmented, fast-moving world. If we get it right, the digital age could be not the end of community, but its next great evolution.

Technology is altering not only how we live and work, but how we are governed. From digital voting systems to AI-driven surveillance, the tools of governance have entered a phase of transformation. While some of these innovations promise greater transparency, participation, and efficiency, others pose serious risks to civil liberties and democratic principles. In this chapter, we explore the evolving intersection between technology and political power— where democracy is being tested and authoritarianism is gaining new tools.

Technology's Impact on Political Systems and Governance

The digital revolution has upended traditional governance structures. Information flows faster, decisions are expected more rapidly, and citizens have unprecedented platforms to voice concerns. Social media, once heralded as a tool for democratization, has become a double-edged sword—spreading both awareness and disinformation at scale.

Digital tools now assist in policy formation, data analysis, and civic engagement. Predictive analytics can help governments anticipate needs. Blockchain technology is being piloted for secure voting systems. Open data initiatives allow greater scrutiny of government spending. These innovations offer promise, but also complexity—what happens when AI influences legislative priorities, or when predictive policing reinforces systemic bias?

Governments must navigate a fine balance. Too slow an adoption of tech, and they risk inefficiency and disconnect. Too fast, and they risk surrendering accountability to opaque algorithms. The evolution of governance requires not only new tools, but new philosophies about representation, agency, and accountability in a digital age.

Surveillance States vs. Democratic Values in Tech Policy

Nowhere is the tension more visible than in the realm of surveillance. The same technologies used to protect citizens—CCTV, biometric databases, facial recognition, geolocation—can also be used to control them. In authoritarian regimes, surveillance has become a central pillar of governance. States like China use AI to monitor online behaviour, assign social credit scores, and suppress dissent with precision.

In democratic countries, the line between safety and surveillance is becoming blurred. The post-9/11 era expanded government monitoring in the name of counterterrorism. Mass data collection, once exceptional, is increasingly normalized. Smart city infrastructure, wearable tech, and mobile apps continuously feed data into central systems. While these tools can enhance public services and urban planning, they also create potential for abuse.

The crucial question is: who watches the watchers? Transparency, judicial oversight, and clear data ethics policies are essential to maintaining democratic accountability. Yet, enforcement remains inconsistent. The push for national security often trumps privacy concerns, even in liberal democracies.

A deeper issue is that surveillance isn't only about data—it's about power. The ability to monitor populations shapes behaviour, silences dissent, and reinforces control. As AI and big data mature, authoritarian regimes gain more refined tools to engineer obedience, while democratic institutions struggle to update outdated legal frameworks.

The Future of Civic Engagement in a Digital Society

While technology can empower authoritarianism, it also offers tools for democratic revitalization. Digital platforms enable grassroots organizing, participatory budgeting, and real-time feedback loops between citizens and representatives. Online petitions, virtual town halls, and decentralized movements challenge traditional hierarchies of influence.

New models of engagement are emerging. Liquid democracy platforms allow citizens to delegate votes on issues to trusted proxies. Blockchain-based voting systems promise security and transparency. Crowdsourced policy platforms gather collective intelligence for law-making. In theory, these tools flatten access to power and reduce corruption.

But digital engagement has limits. Algorithmic feeds create echo chambers, where exposure to opposing views is reduced. Online activism can be performative—hashtags without action. Bots and coordinated misinformation campaigns skew public discourse. Moreover, access remains unequal—many communities still face digital exclusion.

Digital citizenship must therefore be more than access to tools; it must involve education in critical thinking, media literacy, and civic responsibility. Platforms must be held to democratic standards. Algorithms should be subject to scrutiny. Engagement should be deep, not just wide.

In this context, civic engagement may not look like traditional voting. It could include participatory AI audits, citizen data trusts, or open-source regulatory frameworks. The future of democracy depends on whether these new forms are embraced and made meaningful.

Predictions for the Evolution of Governance Styles

The path forward is not fixed. Technological capability will continue to expand, but its application depends on human decisions. Will we see a global drift toward technocracy—rule by experts and data—or a resurgence of local, participatory governance? Will states converge in their use of tech, or will divides widen between digital democracies and surveillance autocracies?

One scenario is hybrid governance—where states adopt sophisticated tech infrastructure but maintain pluralist structures. Here, AI aids public policy, but human rights frameworks guide implementation. Citizens participate in tech oversight through civic councils or algorithmic review boards.

Another scenario is techno-authoritarianism—efficient, centralized systems that deliver public goods but eliminate dissent. This model appeals to regimes that value control over freedom, and to populations that prioritize stability over liberty. Its risk lies in entrenching power, stifling innovation, and eroding rights.

Conversely, digital anarchism could gain traction—decentralized systems where governance is distributed across blockchain protocols, autonomous organizations, and peer-to-peer networks. While this promises autonomy, it also raises issues of coordination, legitimacy, and regulation.

A key factor in all scenarios is the role of corporations. Tech giants already wield more data and influence than many governments. Their platforms shape elections, narratives, and access to knowledge. Whether these entities are brought under democratic control—or become de facto governing institutions—will shape future political landscapes.

Public trust will also be decisive. If citizens believe institutions act in their interest, they may embrace digital governance. If not, disillusionment could foster radical alternatives. Climate change, migration, pandemics, and economic shifts will stress governance systems. Resilience will depend on adaptability, inclusion, and legitimacy.

Final Thoughts

Technology is not neutral—it reflects the values of those who build and wield it. As digital tools become core to governance, we must ask whose values are embedded in code, whose interests are served by algorithms, and whose voices are included in decision-making.

The future of governance is not a binary between democracy and authoritarianism, but a spectrum of possibilities shaped by policy, culture, and public will. The challenge is to build systems that are not only efficient, but just. That empower rather than control. That reflect the messy, diverse, and dynamic nature of human societies.

The digital age demands new visions of leadership, participation, and accountability. It's not enough to digitize old structures—we must reimagine governance for a world where power flows through fibre optics as much as ballot boxes. The choices we make now will determine whether technology becomes a tool of liberation or domination.

And in that, the future is still ours to shape.

The arc of history bends not by chance but by collective will, guided by the choices we make in response to the possibilities and threats ahead. As we stand at a crossroads shaped by unprecedented technological advances, global interconnectedness, environmental crises, and social upheaval, the future feels both more open and more uncertain than ever before. In this concluding chapter, we reflect on the themes explored throughout this book and offer a compass for navigating the road ahead.

Recap of Potential Futures: Utopia, Dystopia, or Somewhere In Between

Every chapter has offered a duality—a fork in the road. In each domain, from artificial intelligence and climate change to the evolution of culture and labour, we have seen how technology and policy can be harnessed to build a better world or ignored to allow systems of oppression, decay, and chaos to flourish.

We've explored utopian scenarios where innovation eradicates poverty, decentralizes power, fosters creativity, and heals the planet. We've also seen the dystopian flipside—where unchecked surveillance, ecological collapse, rampant inequality, and dehumanizing automation turn possibility into peril. And most compellingly, we've dwelled in the in-between: the complex, contradictory present where real-world choices steer outcomes gradually but significantly.

Reality is rarely binary. More often than not, the future unfolds in shades of grey. The challenge is not just to dream of utopia or fear dystopia, but to recognize the incremental ways our current decisions ripple into long-term consequences. The future is being written not by some abstract force, but by billions of actions taken daily—policies enacted, technologies developed, values reinforced or questioned.

The Importance of Responsible Choices Today for a Better Tomorrow

Each domain—whether it concerns health, environment, employment, or governance—demands urgent yet thoughtful responses. But urgency must not lead to panic or authoritarianism. It must inspire ethical innovation, inclusive dialogue, and sustained commitment to equity and sustainability.

When we allow convenience, efficiency, or profit to outweigh human dignity and ecological balance, we edge toward collapse. When we prioritize curiosity, compassion, and collaboration, we move toward renewal. The future will not be handed to us—it must be earned, co-created, and continually re-evaluated.

This means asking better questions. Are we building technologies to liberate or to control? Are we designing systems to empower communities or concentrate power? Are we measuring progress by GDP or by human flourishing? Are we educating for compliance or for wisdom?

It also means making brave decisions. Phasing out fossil fuels despite resistance. Regulating tech monopolies in the face of immense lobbying power. Rethinking education to foster lifelong adaptability. Ensuring access to healthcare and housing as human rights. These are not just policy choices—they are moral commitments.

Call for Collective Reflection and Action Toward a Desirable Future

While technological innovation often commands attention, it is human intention that ultimately directs its course. In this light, collective reflection becomes as important as collective action. We must create spaces—physical and digital, personal and political—where people can grapple with uncertainty, examine their values, and imagine futures worth striving for.

Such reflection is not passive. It's an act of courage in a world that often rewards speed over depth. And it leads directly to action: grassroots organizing, civic participation, community resilience projects, ethical entrepreneurship, and education reform.

We also need to resist cynicism. The idea that "nothing will ever change" is a luxury for those insulated from crisis and a curse for those who suffer under systems that demand change. History teaches us that radical transformation—good or bad—is always possible. That knowledge should embolden us, not paralyze us.

The fork in the road isn't just about grand narratives. It's about everyday decisions: how we treat others, what we consume, how we use our time, and what we choose to believe. Cultural shifts often precede political ones, and imagination fuels both.

The Role of Humanity in Shaping the Being and Becoming of Civilization

Perhaps the central insight from this book is that civilization is not a fixed structure but a living process. We are not passive passengers; we are co-authors. Our technologies, economies, cities, and ideologies are extensions of our collective psyche. When we fear the future, we are often fearing our own reflection in the mirror of invention.

The question, then, is not just what kind of future is possible, but what kind of humans we are choosing to become. Will we be stewards or consumers? Collaborators or conquerors? Citizens or subjects? The answer lies in our capacity for empathy, foresight, and humility.

The 21st century may be remembered as the age when we reached beyond the planet, blurred the line between human and machine, and redefined the limits of life itself. But whether it is remembered as an era of awakening or collapse depends on our collective moral imagination.

What we need now is not merely smarter systems, but wiser societies. Not only technological breakthroughs, but cultural ones. Not just survival, but significance.

As we stand at this fork in the road, let us choose with clarity. Let us embrace complexity without retreating into despair. Let us act not only out of fear of what could go wrong, but out of hope for what could go right. The future is not something that happens to us. It is something we shape—together.

Final Thought

The fork in the road is not a one-time decision. It is a daily, collective journey of becoming. Our role is not simply to react to the future, but to participate in its creation—guided by conscience, driven by curiosity, and rooted in community.

In the end, the most powerful technology we possess is not digital or mechanical. It is human: our ability to imagine, to empathize, to organize, and to endure.

Let us use it well.

Kevian was born in England and has lived in Australia and Asia. Having previously worked as a radio presenter, professional footballer, and Senior multimedia developer, he now creates AI Art and works as a Digital Skills Tutor and Brand Manager. Since 2020, Kevian has been writing novels and exploring new technology to enhance his knowledge and creative journey.

Portfolio: www.kevian.co.uk
Email: kevianauthor@gmail.com

Professional Experience

1. Radio Presenter
Hosted live shows, interviews, and music programmes.
Built strong public speaking and engagement skills.
2. Professional Footballer
Played at a competitive level, demonstrating discipline and teamwork.
3. Senior Multimedia Developer
Developed engaging multimedia content, leading creative teams.
Specialised in visual effects, digital storytelling, and interactive experiences.
4. Digital Skills Tutor
Currently mentoring students in digital technologies, AI, and creative tools.
Focuses on building skills in digital media, web development, and AI art.
5. Brand Manager
Works with businesses to strengthen their online presence and digital identity.
Guides companies through strategic branding initiatives using modern technology.

6. AI Consultant
AI Art, Marketing, Design, Prompt Engineering, Video Production expert.

Creative Works
AI Art
Kevian is passionate about using AI to create visually stunning pieces of art. His works explore the fusion of technology and creativity, pushing boundaries in digital expression.
www.kevian-art.com

www.ingramcontent.com/pod-product-compliance
Lightning Source LLC
LaVergne TN
LVHW051345050326
832903LV00031B/3751